THE COMA WHISPERER

A story based on actual events by

Susan Fox
Avon, Ohio

For information address: Susan Fox, PO Box 421, Avon, Ohio, 44011. Contact Susan via email at brainviewtraininginstitute@gmail.com.

Library of Congress Control Number: 2020904134
Paperback ISBN: 978-1-7346806-0-7
E-book ISBN: 978-1-7346806-1-4
Revised Edition: February 23, 2020

For information about special sales and premium corporate purchases, please call 740-531-0400 24/7 and leave a message with complete contact information. Susan will return the call usually within 24 hours.

Printed in the United States of America

# DISCLAIMER and NOTICE

This book intends to provide accurate, constructive, reliable, useful information in regard to the covered subject matter. It is sold with the understanding that the author is neither engaged in rendering any professional counseling, legal, medical, psychiatric, psychological, spiritual advice or service. If counseling, legal, medical, psychiatric, psychological or spiritual assistance is required, the services of these professionals must be sought elsewhere than from this material.

This is an informational book only. The author guarantees, warranties nothing, nor makes representations of any kind. All covered material is believed to be accurate, constructive, reliable and useful as of the report's writing date. However, no guarantee or warranty is expressed or implied, nor can or will the author be responsible for the business dealings, actions or reliability of any of the report's listed sources provided herein. You agree to read and use this material at your own risk and agree to hold Susan Fox harmless as a result of reading or using this material.

Conduct your own research carefully when reading and learning from any self-help report. You agree that the author of this report shall neither have liability or responsibility to anyone with respect to contacts, negotiations, or agreements that may result from information in this report, or for any loss or damage caused or alleged to have been caused directly or indirectly by such information.

## DEDICATION

This book is dedicated to Love. Love is the frequency of Eternal Life.

Without Love there would be no Life.

# Introduction

When I first saw Jonathan lying motionless on the hospital bed, a shock ran through me. I argued with God in my mind that I couldn't do anything to help him. I wanted to run away. Just a few years earlier, I watched my twelve-year-old son Jason die of a rare birth disorder. I suppressed my urge to let panic drive me away. I believe God gave me a gift to keep working through suppressed grief about losing my only child. I desired to stay strong for Jonathan.

After having four near-death and out of body experiences, I resonate with what many spiritual coaches tell us - we are all immortal, spiritual beings experiencing life as a human. In other words, we are highly intelligent spiritual beings AND human beings in one. Some of us seem to resonate more with our spiritual nature than our human nature. Somehow, I am able to tune in to life on earth with the spiritual part of me more readily than I do with the human side of me. I consider myself to be a spiritual conduit.

As a spiritual channel, I have seen angels, talked to dead people and sent them to the light. I have assisted thousands of people in the end-of-life experience discover how to find peace and hope in their unique and sometimes unimaginably frightening life situations.

I know what feeling hopeless is. I saw it in the mirror when I looked at my bloodshot eyes from crying. I've seen it in the eyes of thousands of stress relief clients. In my experience, I've discovered that natural methods can support the return to wellness. These methods can and do dry your tears and restore a smile to your face.

Are you a mother, father, wife, husband, etc. of a loved one in a coma? What matters most to you regarding your current situation? Would you like to walk into the hospital room and see a new peacefulness in your comatose loved one? If so, be of good cheer. Sometimes miracles come in the most unexpected ways!

Medical science partnered with natural wellness techniques supports and can cause peaceful body responses. Science and metaphysics agree that hearing remains active in comatose cases. Jonathan's conscious responses to my hypnotic suggestions validated this scientific finding.

This book contains Jonathan's story. Based on actual events, I used hypnosis and it helped him come out of his unconscious state. Through hypnosis, sweet Jonathan was able to communicate using his beautiful smile, changing his respiration rate and by blinking his eyelids.

Busy traditional medical doctors can't know every way to work with those in a coma. Some dismiss alternative medicine methods as stress relief possibilities for improving a patient's life. For doctors that only want to rely on traditional medical techniques, you as the caregiver need to be aware. Using this awareness to a medical doctor's experience and training limits, I encourage you to be bold. Be open to making decisions a medical doctor may deem unsuitable to consider. You never know what natural approach might improve your comatose loved one's life quality.

I encourage you to search for new approaches, even ones a traditional medical doctor might dismiss as frivolous. If it causes no harm, why not check it out?

Are you willing to using a complementary alternative that's different from what's familiar yet proven to work with others for this type of situation? Willing to face your fear of doing something new and different? If you want to help your unconscious loved one reduce stress and communicate using proven-effective and safe hypnosis, this book can open your eyes to new chances. Alternative medicine practitioners can be an answer to making things better for your unique situation.

I've worked with people globally. Somehow, people find me by referral. Since working with Jonathan, I've worked with several people in coma and stroke recovery. Using thinking strategies, gentle mind and brain exercises, hypnosis, Reiki and the ancient universal art of releasing tension called Jin Shin Jyutsu, I now help people reduce their stress using many techniques. Together, we develop positive thinking strategies to transform what seems impossible into the possible.

This transformation comes as a result of understanding that believing is seeing. When you BELIEVE in an idea, whether it be true or false, you get the result in which you believe. Believe a situation is hopeless, and you get a pessimistic conclusion. Conversely, believe in what is possible and you get miracles.

After my experience with Jonathan, I learned that seeing a situation from the love in your heart gives you hope. I learned that fear and sadness can ruin your life if you let it. Feeling hopeful is a good habit to develop.

I am not afraid to die because I personally know we do not die. Instead, we complete our journey on earth and continue living in a different realm. When Jason completed his journey here, his spirit separated from his physical body. He continues to live in a different place now. The same is true for all of us. I am grateful for the opportunity to help my clients find out how to live in the love light instead of in fear.

If you are looking to feel hopeful, to be a part of a miracle, you've come to the right place. Believing IS seeing. I look forward to us traveling this journey together to see what IS possible for you and your loved one.

Sincerely hopeful,
Susan

Chapter One
The Outing

Jonathan Wallace had always loved the church's picnics. He and his best friend Joey Shiloh enjoyed running around the park with the other children just being kids.

"Grandma! Look at me! I'm a jumping bean!" beamed Nancy Wallace's grandson, Jonathan. She smiled while watching her eight-year-old little dynamo exude boundless energy as he boinged across the picnic area.

"Oh, I bet you can jump higher than that!" encouraged Grandma Nancy.

Publicly tossing down the high jump challenge gauntlet, Jonathan imagined himself doing even better.

"Now watch me, Grandma! I've just blasted off my shoe rockets!"

More boinging bubbled up in this creative little guy. This time Jonathan jumped just a little bit higher. For Grandma, his greatest fan, he'd gladly jump to the moon if he could.

"Wow! It's a good thing you have shoe rockets. No one can catch you now!"

Grandma smiled broadly playing into Jonathan's super boy fantasy. She divided her attention between watching Rocket Boy and taking out picnic items from a box. Setting a homemade, scrumptious Dutch apple pie on a nearby picnic table she said, "How many boings can you count before your head touches the trees?"

"One, two, three…" started counting Jonathan. He boinged until he saw Joey show up. "Hey, Grandma. Joey's here. I'm going to have a jumping contest with him. I'll be right back."

"Okay, but stay where I can see you."

With that, Jonathan boinged over to where Joey was standing just outside his parent's van. Joey had something in his hand.

"Look, I have this."

"What is it?" Jonathan stopped boinging to study it for a minute.

"It's a rock from outer space."

Jonathan tilted his head and closely examined what looked like a rock with deep crevasses and jagged cracks in it. "How do you know it's from outer space?"

"Well, doesn't it LOOK like it's from outer space?" said Joey who was a more gullible eight-year-old than Jonathan.

"Naw! It looks like it's from earth. I think it's dinosaur doo-doo."

Bringing it closer to his face, Joey eyed the object more discreetly. "Dinosaur doo-doo?!"

"Just kidding." said Jonathan with a snicker. "Who told you it was from outer space?"

"My big brother Bill."

Jonathan was quiet for a minute. "Is this the same brother that told you when you cut your finger and it heals, the dried blood disappears into another world?"

"Yes."

"Okay." agreed Jonathan. That was all he needed to hear. "Maybe it is from outer space."

"You really think it is?!" wondered Joey.

"NO! I think your brother Bill is trying to trick you." said Jonathan who always acted like a loving brother to Joey. "But we can pretend it's from outer space if you'd like…"

The two boys laughed.

"Look, Joey, I'm a jumping bean." said Jonathan and he started boinging up and down again.

Joey started flapping his arms like a bird and wriggling his upper torso around in a snakelike fashion as he jumped up and down, too. He looked like somebody had plugged him into an electrical light socket. "Me, too! I'm a jumping bean. And I can jump higher than you!"

The two boys laughed and giggled like little girls. Nancy Wallace looked over at them and felt a warm spot spread in her heart. Watching Jonathan innocently playing with Joey reminded her of last year at the picnic.

Both boys had imaginary friends then. Joey and Jonathan had been playing super heroes. They had been working hard saving the world from the evil giant gorilla who was trying to scare the picnickers. Together with the help of Joey's invisible friend named Michael and Ryan, Jonathan's invisible friend, they were shooing off this big, horrible, hairy monkey. They ran around waving their arms in the air and using shot off invisible bazookas to scare away the invisible ape.

In her memory, she eventually recalled Jonathan all sweaty and red-faced coming up to her husband Tim. He and Joey had been running here and there through the picnic area. Jonathan asked Grandpa Tim for a drink refill.

"Grandpa Tim? Would you give my friend Ryan another glass of lemonade? We're parched after chasing off Ooga Booga."

"Ooga Booga?"

"Yes. He's that big hairy ape that's been bothering everyone. But we made him go away because we are super heroes."

"I see…" said Tim hiding a smile.

Jonathan smiled at Grandpa Tim barely exposing two upper front teeth just beginning to emerge.

"Are you sure Ryan really wants more lemonade? Hasn't he already had two cupsful?" Tim asked.

Nancy loved that Tim played along in the fun. Tim was a much more laid-back grandparent to Jonathan than he was as a parent to their son David.

Jonathan stood there for a moment with hopeful eyes, holding up an empty plastic cup to his grandfather. "Maybe just half a cup. If Ryan wants more, he can always come back. Okay, Buddy?"

"Okay, Grandpa." agreed Jonathan.

Grandpa walked over to the 5-gallon cooler and measured out about 3 ounces of icy yellow liquid. Then, Joey held his empty cup up to Mr. Wallace.

"Michael wants some, too." Tim smiled and pushed in the cooler can's button again, releasing about a half cup of lemonade for "Michael", too. Then Tim looked over at his wife, Nancy. "I think Michael and Ryan are thirstier than Joey and Jonathan!"

Joey and Jonathan looked at each other and then in unison said, "We want some more!" With that, Tim poured each of them another half cup of liquid. They drank the refreshing fluid and went back to playing their imaginary game saving the picnickers from the evildoer nobody could see.

"Nancy? What do you want? A hamburger? A hot dog? What?" asked the barbecue chef.

"What?" said Nancy being shaken from her memory.

"We need a count. Burger or dog?"

"Oh, a hamburger would be great." she said zooming forward to the present day. The delicious grilling smells triggered her stomach to growl.

"I'm hungry, too." said her friend Ben who stood near her.

Nancy sheepishly smiled. "Nothing like the great outdoors to give you a hearty appetite." she offered.

Soon, the grill chef started loading cooked delicacies into some nearby pans. Charlie Jamison and Joan Seymore, church board members, used aluminum foil to cover two big pans piled high with barbecued meat. Covering the pans with foil seemed like such an obvious thing to do to keep the nasty flies from nibbling on the aromatic meat. But at times, what may seem obvious to one person is an ingenuous idea to another.

"Dogs and burgers are ready!" yelled Charlie from underneath the picnic shelter.

"Come and get it!" he bellowed loudly so church members further away could hear.

Three-year-old Brittany scrambled off her mother's lap. "Mommy!" she excitedly proclaimed, "Hot dogs!" She clapped her hands and enthusiastically added, "Ketchup!" as she made a beeline for the food.

Young boys dashed to the front of the line. You could almost see their eyes cartoonishly bulge out of their eye sockets with hunger.

"Before we eat, we'll ask for God's blessings on our food. Pastor?" asked Charlie looking toward the minister.

Everyone bowed their head as Pastor Jenkins offered a prayer over the meal. After the prayer, adults and children alike happily visited with each other as they chowed down on some tasty morsels.

Ben Michaels, the church organist and Nancy Wallace, the choir director, stood in line chit chatting and putting food on their plates.

"Mmmmm. It smells heavenly!" said Nancy.

Ben smiled at Nancy's remarks. A beautiful, feminine, friendly woman everyone liked, Nancy was sometimes outspoken. A genuine laugh engaged those around her attracting men, women and children alike. Ben liked that attractive, contagious laughing quality in Nancy.

The two grownups carried their lunch and sat down at a nearby picnic table. They sat across from Nancy's grandson and his best friend Joey.

"Don't take this the wrong way, but it seems strange to see you without Rose. How long has she been gone now?"

"Only a week. It DOES feel strange for her to be gone. But they'll be back in September. I'm jealous and I'm not. She is so lucky she got to go to Europe with her granddaughter."

"Yes. She was really lucky to win that trip."

"I got a post card from her and Tammy just today. She sent me a picture of a castle the two of them had visited in Edinburgh, Scotland."

"Amazing to think people lived in castles and that they are still standing in some parts of the world."

"September can't come soon enough for me. I know it's selfish of me to want her back right away. But I miss talking with her. Did you know we sometimes talk on the phone two or three times a day? And she only lives a couple of blocks away from me!"

"She's a good friend to you."

"She's my best friend!"

"You two do seem like two peas in a pod."

"Exactly."

"Why didn't you go with her to Europe?"

"I won't get on an airplane. Scared to death to fly on those contraptions."

"Ah, she couldn't talk you into it."

"Never!"

"Hey, any changes in Tim's brother?" said Ben to Nancy. "He went to visit Phil today, didn't he?" Ben was Tim's dearest childhood friend.

"My husband is so good to Phil. If only he didn't have Alzheimer's. Goodness, it's hard for me to cheer Tim up after he gets back from the nursing home. What a horrible disease..." Nancy's voice trailed off as she refocused her conscious concentration on a spontaneously triggered, internal "before" and "now" memory about Phil.

"Hand me that paint scraper, Tim."

"Here ya go, Phil."

"I think this 30-year layer of paint is all that's keeping your porch ceiling together. What's wrong with you letting this get so rotted up in here?"

"I knew we were going to paint soon. I saved it just for you because I love to hear you complain." mused Tim.

Phil darted a disapproving glare toward his sibling. "I'm going to ignore that remark because it's not worth acknowledging."

"I'm doing work!" announced four-year-old Jonathan as he busied himself with his plastic tools set. He pounded on the bottom of the front screen door Nancy had precariously tilted in her lap. She was almost done sanding off the old paint preparing it for a new color.

Nancy smiled lovingly at her grandson. "And you're doing a fine job of it, too."

Jonathan beamed with importance. Grandma's praise confirmed his obviously valued contribution to the family's project. At least in Jonathan's mind...

Phil and Tim stopped for a moment and chuckled at Jonathan. Then, the two men still briefly grinning at Jonathan's innocent remark, resumed their own conversation.

"Aha, Phil, but saying you're going to ignore my remark is actually acknowledging my remark."

"Is not!" objected Phil turning back to the porch ceiling.

"Is, too!" Tim waited before saying anything else for a minute. Then he blurted, "Oh, never mind. Just focus on fixing the rotted wood Your Mighty Flatulence." Tim pasted a know-it-all smile on his face waiting for Phil to turn back around and look at him.

Phil turned and rolled his eyes while looking at Tim again. "I AM focusing on what I'm doing."

"No, you're not. You're complaining about what you're doing. Complaining is not doing."

"If I was complaining you'd know it. Remember that time I complained that the wind was purposely sneaking up on that hot dog wrapper at the park when we were kids? *That* was me complaining."

"Yeah. You were complaining. And, it was too funny." agreed Tim. "Just when you got close enough to grab that hot dog wrapper, the wind came along and moved it just out of your reach again."

"I couldn't grab it. It frustrated the heck out of me."

"Focusing on what you can't do just keeps you stuck in life."

"I know that. That's why I just let that wrapper go. I wasn't going to let it get the best of me. That's why I just sat down on the bench and 'oh welled' it."

"'Oh welled' it?"

"Yeah, you know. I just said, 'Oh well.' I had done my best to get the wrapper and couldn't get it. I accepted that my destiny at that moment was simply to sit down, eat the dog and drink my soda."

"But you didn't really like it because you're such a perfectionist. It really rubbed you the wrong way at first because you love to keep your yard so pristine."

"Are you going to point out all the things you don't like about me or are we going to get back to work?"

"Sure, why not? That's what brothers do, don't they?"

"It doesn't do any good to focus on the past right now when we've got a job to do. The sky's starting to gray up. Do you want my help right now or don't cha?"

"Well, let's just take a little break. We've been going at it for a while now. What say we stop and have a lemonade?"

"Hey, I've only got 32 minutes left. I have other things I want to do today besides your porch." said Phil, obviously annoyed at Tim's ribbing.

"You're complaining again…"

"I'm going to ignore that remark."

"Didn't we already see this movie?"

Nancy chuckled remembering that conversation between the two loving brothers. She contrasted it with a present flashback memory of Phil.

In the brief current nursing home memory Tim and she had come to visit Phil. Phil recognized Nancy and Tim and sat down in the day room next to them. Within about a minute, he absorbed himself in watching TV, got up and walked out of the room. He forgot Tim and Nancy were even there.

Recalling the day room scenario, Nancy sighed as a tear welled up in her eye. Lingering in the memory for a moment, she unexpectedly found herself transported back to the picnic.

"Mrs. Wallace?" abruptly called one of the children to Nancy who felt a ball bounce up against her leg.

"Mrs. Wallace? Would you throw us the ball?"

"Huh?"

Nancy looked down at the cement floor. There was a red plastic ball loosely rolling around.

"Oh, sure." she reached down, picked up the ball and tossed it to a little boy.

"Thanks, Mrs. Wallace."

Ben had seen Nancy's momentary faraway look on her face. Like her husband Tim, she, too, felt sad that her brother-in-law was only a mere shell of a man now.

"Yeah. That's sad." said Ben mechanically looking at Nancy's face. He felt like he had just poured salt on an open wound.  Shouldn't have opened that door thought Ben wondering how to fill the uncomfortable immediate silence.

"Well... how about your grandson Jonathan?  He's such a bright little guy.  He sure knows a lot about fishing."

Jonathan put a potato chip in his mouth and crunched it. He looked at Ben when he heard his name.  "Yep!  I love to sit by the river and get those fish."

"Me, too." chimed in Joey.

Nancy brightened a bit.  "Yes, he and Tim have given us many delicious fish dinners."  Nancy smiled as she looked at Jonathan sitting across from her at the same picnic table.

Jonathan stuffed a two-bite piece of hotdog into his mouth. Ketchup and mustard squeezed out the corners of his mouth.  He was making faces at Joey.  Joey was laughing and pointing at Jonathan's cheeks.  His face looked like a squirrel's jammed with acorns.

"Jonathan, stop playing with your food." said Nancy.

Jonathan loved Grandma and Grandpa Wallace.  They treated him with great respect and kindness.  Jonathan looked in Grandma's direction and replied with a defeated, "Okaaaay."  Joey bent his head down in shame for a moment.  Both the boys knew better than to joke around during meals.

Nancy shifted her weight from one butt cheek to the other.

"Nancy, you look like you're doin' a chair dance."

"This picnic bench feels like it's got nails in it.  If I was one of those Indian swami's I might like it but I'm just an old lady who prefers comfort."

"I'm with you.  Either my butt has gotten bonier or this bench has gotten harder." joked Ben.

Nancy chuckled.  She got up and moved a couple of feet away from Jonathan and Joey to a more comfortable looking folding chair.  Ben liked that idea and followed her with his food to an empty chair near Nancy's.

Jonathan and Joey continued to eat and giggle through lunch.  Watching Jonathan innocently play reminded Nancy of the day he was born.  This was her first grandson.  He held a special place in her heart, especially now after what had happened to David and Phoebe, Jonathan's parents.

Nancy remembered the day Jonathan was born.

"Push!"

"I'm too tired to push anymore!" cried out Phoebe, Jonathan's mother. "I want somebody else to take over! Just get this baby out of me!" she exhaustedly pled.

"Phoebe!" insisted Nancy to her daughter-in-law. "You can do this. You're almost there. And when you're done, you'll have a wonderful, darling baby for all your work."

"I can't! I'm done! I have nothing left..." moaned Phoebe.

Nancy stroked Phoebe's profusely sweating forehead while David, her adoring husband and Nancy's only son, held her hand.

"Honey, you CAN do this." contended Nancy. "Did you hear the doctor? The doctor can see the baby's head. That means he's almost here."

"Sweetheart," said David. "I know you're tired. But I believe in you. You can do this!"

"You! You did this to me! Get away from me! Don't ever touch me again!" fussed Phoebe at David.

"ME?! Hey, this was a joint decision. Now stop being a big baby and PUSH!"

With fire in her eyes she glared at David. And then, in unison with another contraction, Phoebe bore down with all her might. Almost instantly, out popped Jonathan's head.

"Just one more push!" enthusiastically encouraged the doctor. "You're almost done."

And with all the strength Phoebe could muster she pushed down hard again. Then, as if by magic, out popped a gorgeous, pink, ten-fingered and ten-toed, healthy baby boy.

David cried. Nancy cried. Tim cried. Even the doctor had a tear in his eye.

"You did it, Sweetheart!" marveled David. "You are amazing."

David leaned down to kiss his adored bride. Nancy and Tim's children had started their family at last, a day long awaited by them all.

Then, the nurse cleaned Jonathan's birth canal goo off and wrapped him in a receiving blanket. Named after Phoebe's father, this special bundle of love arrived crying on his own.

"Now that's a healthy set of lungs on my boy!" beamed David. Congratulations were shared all around and soon everyone dried their elated joyful tears at his arrival.

Jonathan opened his eyes and stretched and yawned a big yawn. As he reached out his tiny arms, they wriggled and jiggled looking a little like the way a fish looks flipping and flapping when it first comes out of the water.

"So THAT'S what he was doing inside me when it seemed like a fish was flopping around inside me. He was stretching his arms!" chuckled Phoebe as she watched the young love of her life visibly stretch his limbs for the first time. Nancy smiled at the memory that was one of the happiest days of her life next to giving birth to David.

"Grandma?" said Jonathan jolting Nancy back to the present-day picnic. "Joey and I are going to the playground. Okay?"

Jonathan had mustard, bits of chocolate cake and ketchup on the front of his shirt.

"Jonathan! Look at your shirt!"

"What?!"

"Your shirt is a mess!"

"Grandma…" calmly began Jonathan. He winked at Joey mouthing 'just a minute' to him and walked over to his grandma. He put his arm around her. "That's just lunch. I'm a little boy. I'm supposed to enjoy life like this."

Nancy grabbed a paper towel from the nearby picnic table and put some spit on it wiping some trace condiments from his face. As she wiped his face, she tried to simultaneously hold back laughter from his remark.

"Aw, Grandma!" he said objecting to her fussing over him. But he really loved it because this was Grandma after all. And he loved the attention.

"We should go home right now and I should put you in the bathtub!"

"But you won't will you because you know I'm a little boy and little boys that you love need to play outside." he said batting his eyes at her lovingly with an impish smile on his face.

"All right. Go on. Make sure it's okay with Joey's parents, too. But stay at the playground where I can still see you. We're only going to be here for another hour or so. Don't make me come looking for you."

"Okay, Grandma."

With that Jonathan kissed Grandma on the cheek and scampered off with Joey to the playground.

"Hey! Go ask Joey's parents first!" Fussed Grandma to the boys. They stopped dead in their tracks and headed over to where Joey's parents were picnicking. When Joey's parents approved of them playing at the playground, the boys skedaddled off toward the playground.

When they were far enough away, Jonathan whispered, "Hey, let's go fishing."

Joey raised his eyebrows and smiled a big smile.

They ran off toward the playground to romp, stomp and get dirty like little boys do. But it was merely for a little while. They had other plans in mind.

An hour or so passed. Nancy started to feel sleepy after eating that big lunch. "Goodness, I think I need a nap."

"Yeah, sounds like a great idea." agreed Ben.

"This fresh open air is making me tired. I think I'm going to get on home before I fall asleep out here."

"Hey, Nancy, it was great seeing you. Sorry I missed Tim. Tell him I'll call him later."

"Will do."

Nancy stood up from the chair and stretched a bit. She looked around for Jonathan.

"Hey, Ben, do you see Jonathan?" Ben stood up and laid his right-hand level above his eyebrows as he scanned the horizon. He was joking with Nancy.

"This Seattle Seahawk doesn't see him at first glance. He's probably with Joey." Nancy glanced sideways at Ben ignoring his poor attempt at humor.

"Hey, Betty, do you see Jonathan?"

"No…" said Nancy's friend sitting under the picnic shelter. "Wasn't he here a minute ago?"

"Yes, but he ran off to play with Joey at the playground."

Some of the other church members sitting near Nancy, Betty and Ben stood up. They scanned the area looking for the two young boys.

Nancy walked out from underneath the picnic shelter toward the playground. Even though she could clearly see in all directions Jonathan was nowhere to be seen, she scanned the area anyway.

*Where is he?* Nancy's heart rate began to quicken. The more she looked for her grandson, the more she noticed he was gone.

The other adult church members started to spontaneously roam the park searching for the boys.

Chapter Two
Jonathan and Grandpa

"Ha, ha…the evil guy Fred is trying to blast the good guys." narrated Jonathan in a fantasized fight pitting six-inch action figures against each other. Splash! He plopped one of the figures into a nearby water puddle.

"Oof!" Jonathan continued the sparring match against the two pieces of extruded plastic.

Oblivious to the beauty all around him in the great outdoors, eight-year-old Jonathan lost himself in his playtime. The rocks, bugs and woods at the Green River in Kanaskat-Palmer State Park served as a great backdrop for the third grader's imaginative melodrama.

As he continued playing while lying on a big, flat rock, the youngster muddied his knees and the front of his red cotton t-shirt.

The first time he and Grandpa Tim had come fishing here, Grandpa said the rock looked like his first car, a 1967 Volkswagen Beetle. From then on, they had called the rock the Volkswagen rock.

The sun beat down on the young nature explorer. "Later on, I might just take a little swim in the river." he said out loud to himself.

He peered over the rock's edge looking into the murky-green river water below. He was looking for Never Quits.

Jonathan watched the sun dance off the fishes' scales as one occasionally popped its head up above the water's surface. As the invincible boy looked mesmerized into the water, his mind faded back to the last fishing trip with Grandpa Tim.

"You see that one monster-size steelhead down there?" said Grandpa.

"Yeah. He's big!"

"Yeah, bigger than the rest. I've been fishing here for 10 years. That same fish has been here all that time."

"How do you know that's the same fish, Grandpa?"

"See that mark on his side?"

Grandpa pointed to a dark spot on the fish that looked like an Indian arrowhead.

"Yes…"

"That's how I know. He's hearty, stout, strong…" said Grandpa forming a fist and flexing his right bicep. Jonathan smiled as he looked at the muscular powerhouse now appearing on Grandpa's arm.

Jonathan flexed his own arm, though puny compared to Grandpa's.

"I'm strong like you, Grandpa."

"Boy…" said Grandpa feeling Jonathan's walnut-sized molehill now visible on the young lad's right upper arm. "I'd be no match for you. You could destroy me with those bruisers if I ever crossed you."

Looking somber and serious, Jonathan said assuredly, "Oh Grandpa…I would never fight you. My muscles are here to protect you if anybody ever tried to hurt us."

Grandpa Tim smiled and winked appreciatively at Jonathan. "That's my boy."

"How long do trout live, Grandpa?"

"Most trout live about 10 years or so. But he just keeps on toughing it out. I've even named him."

"What's his name? Does he come to you when you call him?"

Grandpa chuckled. "I named him Never Quits. But I don't call to him. He just keeps showing up pretty much in this same spot. He never gives up. I guess he's still got plenty of living to do."

"Yeah."

"Now let's stop talking. Too much talkin' let's the fish know we are here. Grandma's favorite dish is fish."

"That's funny, Grandpa. Dish is fish."

"Guess I'm a poet but I know it."

The two guys snickered.

"Let's get some fish for Grandma, Jonathan. She likes that. One time I caught a fish for Grandma that was almost as big as you."

"You did?!?"

"Uh huh. It was when we were in high school together. A bunch of us went out for the day fishing. I even have a picture of it somewhere if I can remember where I put it."

"Is the picture at home?"

"Yeah. Somewhere. Maybe it's in the attic. Remind me to show you when we get home. You might have to help me find it."

"Boy, I'd like to see that!"

"Me, too. It's been a while since I've seen that picture of me standing with Grandma and that big fish. You'll see."

"Yeah. We like to make Grandma smile. We can do it with a fish!"

Grandpa chuckled again, smiling at his grandson.

Then, Jonathan shook himself from his fond fishing recollection with Grandpa.

"So, you think you can escape me, Never Quits?" boldly dared Jonathan looking at the famous fish. He darted his arms teasingly toward the swimming creatures submerged safely below the water.

"Have to get closer to catch one of you slippery monsters."

He lay on the rock picturing himself scooping up a fish using the ball cap he was wearing. In his vision, he saw himself as a super-hero with bulging biceps. He effortlessly dunked his cap into the cold, rushing, white water below and snagged a fish. Wouldn't Grandma Nancy and Grandpa Tim be impressed when he came home with a great big trout dinner? It would be even better if his catch was the most famous fish!

Though actually, the fish were just out of reach, the fifty-seven-pound hero didn't let that stop him. He could easily get closer to the water to grab one of those slick, scaly, silvery-green prizes.

"I just need to move a little closer to them." said Jonathan as he scooted his butt and hands along closer to the edge of the big, flat rock.

Closer to the water, he carefully sat up and then swung his legs over the edge.

"Rats! If only I could stretch my legs out like Expando-Man." he said out loud briefly imagining a scene with his plastic superhero figures again.

"Wait, I'll just roll over on my belly." he said as he moved himself nearer to the rocks below.

Turning his body over, he laid down and scraped his chin on the warm rock. He skinned his knee a bit, too, when he turned over but he refused to let that stop him.

"I'm Never Quits. I'm almost there."

He moved the lower half of his body down closer to the water.

Holding his ball cap in one hand, he grabbed a jagged part of the Volkswagen rock with the other. He moved his body down about two feet toward the mossy-covered boulder below.

"Where is that rock?" he said dangling his right foot just above where he pictured the stone landing beneath must be. Rather than actually look where the stone was, he kept moving toward where he imagined it to be. But then he started slipping.

"Whoops!" Faster than he could believe, he slid out of control. Into the fast-moving, cold, blue liquid he plunked. He tore his chin further on the rocks before he plopped like a brick into the rushing river water.

"Help!" he wailed in panicked despair as he bobbed up for a moment. But nobody was around to hear him. His arms and legs flailing haphazardly in the clutches of this very real nightmare, he dunked under the water again.

He thrashed against the chilly, aquamarine companion. He sputtered water out of his mouth as the water kept intruding in. "Help! Grandma! This way." he cried out again.

Up into his nose went the unwanted, wet intruder. He choked on incoming water, struggling to breathe. With lightning speed, the swift moving waves took him along for a ride he'd never imagined.

"Grambufgy." he continued to do his best to call Grandma's name with water coming in fast. He started to feel like a campfire being drowned by a bucket of water. No! This couldn't be happening to him. He was a strong swimmer. *Grandma will be here soon.*

His body careened down the river. He thought his luck had changed for a moment as he grabbed on to some branches. But as he seized a branch, it broke away. He floated helplessly down the river again and got caught in some submerged branches that trapped and imprisoned him.

Soon, this forty-five-inch tall boy was looking up from underneath the water. His arms and legs barely moved as more water filled his lungs.

"Grandma, here I am!" he weakly and silently called one more time in vain. When there was nothing else left, he could do, he unwillingly surrendered to the unstoppable, incoming rush of splash.

The cold liquid was an unmanageable torrent of hopelessness that flooded his lungs. His mind's last image was of the one person he trusted more than anyone except Grandpa Tim. The final word that escaped from his frozen, blue lips was, "Grandma." Unconscious now, he'd careened out of control into a web of lifeless, submerged tree branches.

Jonathan was dead. And nobody knew where he was.

Then, Jonathan's spirit seemed to lift up out of his body. It felt strange because he could breathe underwater while at the same time, he saw his lifeless body still being held captive by a network of branches. He came up out of the water and scampered up onto the shore.

He could see adult church members frantically yelling for him. It was all so confusing for him.

"Jonathan! Joey!" the quickly organized search party yelled out. Jonathan's spirit could hear them calling to him.

"I'm here." he shouted at the top of his lungs, but nobody could seem to hear him. He ran toward Grandma and stood right in front of her. "Grandma!" said Jonathan's spirit waving his hands in front of her face and jumping up and down trying to get her attention. But she never acknowledged him.

She joined the adults who roamed unsystematically through the park still calling to Jonathan and Joey. Almost 20 minutes had passed since anyone had remembered seeing Jonathan.

"Is Joey missing, too?" wondered Jonathan in spirit form. "He's not in the water. I wonder where he is?"

Jonathan stood right next to his grandmother. She stood with her hands on her hips, scanning the horizon. "Who's that?" she wondered out loud looking at a small figure skipping merrily toward her.

"Look everyone. I caught a frog and I found a snake stick."

"Joey, where's Jonathan?" said Grandma to Joey. She reached out and hugged him glad to see he was all right.

"Jonathan? I don't know. I was playing in the mud over by that big tree." Joey pointed to a huge Blue Spruce. "I started counting for hide and seek. Jonathan hid. But I couldn't find him. So, I just started playing by myself. See my stick?" Joey said holding a small stick up to Nancy's face.

"It kind of looks like a snake, doesn't it?" said Joey in wonder.

"Joey!" shouted Jonathan's spirit at Joey. Again, Jonathan's spirit jumped up and down waving his arms at his best buddy. "I'm here! Can't you see me?" but Joey seemed to be ignoring his best friend.

A young fifty-something Grandma, Nancy had a level head on her shoulders. She had a seamstress business and was very successful at it. She was good at figuring things out but she started to feel concerned about Jonathan's absence.

"Last year, we found Joey and Jonathan playing inside a box underneath a tablecloth. Jonathan's got to be here somewhere." calmly said Nancy.

"Of course, he's here. He's fine. We'll find him." assured Ben. He tussled Joey's hair also glad to see he was all right.

The adults kept looking. After ten minutes of Jonathan being absent, Nancy began to feel concerned.

"Did anyone look in the parking lot? Maybe Jonathan's in somebody's car or van."

Just then, Joey's parents walked up and said, "Joey! Where have you been? We've been worried sick about you!" They both grabbed him and held their child close.

"We just came from the parking lot. No sign of Jonathan as far as we could see."

Then, Nancy said, "This is really strange that Jonathan's not here."

Some more church members came walking up from the direction of the yurts, shelters and cabins. "There was no sign of Jonathan at the camping ground yurts, cabins or shelters. We called and called to him but he never answered." Relieved to see Joey, the church members smiled at the young boy.

"I don't think we can wait any longer to see what kind of mischief he's gotten into this year. Now I'm getting worried." declared Nancy. She started looking pale.

"I think we should call in the park ranger, Ben."

"I agree." He started toward the ranger tower, but Nancy stopped him. She motioned to another church member who stood several feet away.

"Joan, would you come here for a minute?" Quickly Joan came over to Nancy.

"I think it's time to get the park ranger involved. I want to keep looking for Jonathan. Do you think you can adequately describe him to the officer?"

"I can do that, but do you have a picture of him?"

"Good idea. I'll go and get it from my purse." Joan and Nancy walked briskly back to the picnic shelter together. Nancy opened her purse and quickly found Jonathan's picture and handed it to Joan.

"Remember, Jonathan's wearing athletic shoes, blue jean cutoffs and a white shirt with a Duck Tales picture on it."

"Got it. We'll find him."

"I know we will. Now go. Thanks, Joan." and with that Ben and Nancy walked in the opposite direction from the ranger station to continue looking for Jonathan.

"I'm worried. I feel like I've lost so much already. I can't lose Jonathan, too." acknowledged Nancy.

"Nancy, I know you've been through a lot. In fact, I marvel at your inner strength. I don't know if I could handle what you've endured over the past ten years." Ben talked with Nancy the way he usually did... in a way that focused on strengths instead of staying stuck in weaknesses.

"But let's wait before we jump to any conclusions. For all we know Jonathan's so immersed in playing somewhere, he's completely oblivious to us looking for him."

"You're a good friend, Ben." Nancy felt a little calmer. Ben could be right. The two adults talked sparsely as they continued looking amongst trees and bushes for the lost little one.

"What I was saying a minute ago. I mean it. I've watched you and Tim along the way and I just don't know how you keep going."

"Ben, it's God. God is my strength. Knowing that God is always here with me, no matter how weak I might be at times, I have a respite from my cares."

Ben seemed to silently look right through Nancy at that moment. Their eyes met somberly. Nancy kept quiet about the worry that was in her mind. But Ben could see it on her face.

"I'm going to look over here." pointed Nancy to a nearby area dense with bushes.

Nancy calmed herself a little as she walked behind the bushy area outside of Ben's sight. She closed her eyes and imagined angels coming to Jonathan's aid. God, if Jonathan's in trouble, please come to his rescue. Bring him what he needs so he can hang on until we find him.

She prayed as she continued searching for her curious little boy. Had his curiosity gotten the best of him?

Standing by a bush that was tucked away near the river, she stopped for a minute cupping her hands to her mouth and shouted, "Jonathan! Jonathan! It's Grandma. Come on out now." She simultaneously looked nowhere and everywhere.

Joey joined in the hunt yelling Jonathan's name, too. "Wait till Jonathan sees my snake stick!" He wished his best friend would come out from his hiding place so they could play once again.

"Boy, Jonathan's gonna be in big, big trouble when we find him." thought Joey to himself out loud.

Jonathan's spirit felt disoriented and confused. "Am I dead?" he wondered. "Am I really dead?"

For a moment Nancy's mind flashed back to a time when four-year-old Jonathan was at home on Albert Street in Wilkeson. In the memory, Nancy and Jonathan snuggled close together on the couch. She had been reading Green Eggs and Ham to him.

She remembered the very warm June weather tiring her. She hadn't had the air conditioner on because it was so expensive to use. Soon, she had nodded off. Before she knew it, her bold pre-school-aged grandson had dashed off the couch.

Quietly he opened the front door, stepped onto the porch and carefully closed the door behind him so it didn't slam. It was boring watching Grandma and Grandpa sleep. He wanted to play.

On that summer day long ago, Nancy recalled dreaming about an angel playing a harp. In the dream Nancy felt comfortable listening to the angel's harp recital. But then, the angel got up from playing and put her hand on Nancy's shoulder. Nancy awoke with a start.

Intuitively upon awakening she looked around the living room while simultaneously trying to get more awake. In his easy chair her husband Tim was snoring so loudly he sounded like a chainsaw. But where was Jonathan?

Then, she realized Jonathan was gone. Like a human being shot from a cannon, she jumped up from the couch and ran outside. There was Jonathan innocently playing in the sandbox with his toys. She sighed a deep sigh of relief. Surely that would be the case now as everyone searched for the older Jonathan missing in the park, wouldn't it?

"Jonathan!" yelled Ben. He started to feel hoarse from all the yelling. Jonathan's spirit came running up to Ben. "Here I am, Mr. Michaels!" Jonathan's spirit waved his hands in front of Mr. Michaels face. But Jonathan was beginning to feel like it was no use. He felt so confused about what was happening. He knew his physical body was under water. What was going on?

Ben Michaels was a retired tree feller. Cutting down probably thousands of trees in his forty-year woodsman career, he was no stranger to the rugged outdoors. His search for Jonathan had led him to one end of the river. He was about fifty feet away from the rest of the group when he saw something about ten feet in from the river's shore.

"Jonathan?" loudly called out Nancy, still looking for her grandson. She stood up and scanned the immediate horizon while simultaneously staying somewhat near Ben's search area.

"I'm right here, Grandma!" insisted Jonathan's spirit as he dashed up beside her. But she couldn't see or hear him.

Nancy stopped for a moment. She felt like someone was standing on her right side. In fact, she could have sworn she heard Jonathan call out, "Grandma! I'm right here!" For an instant she felt strangely peaceful. But she dismissed the idea thinking she was just imagining it.

Nancy didn't really understand the feeling she felt. Looking around thinking that Jonathan stood nearby, she was communicating with his spirit on an invisible level. She just didn't know it yet.

Then, Nancy turned slightly to her left. She noticed Ben moving closer to the river.

If anyone can find Jonathan, it will be Ben Nancy thought to herself. Oh, Rose and Tim, I really wish you were here with me now!

Suddenly, Ben darted closer to the river.

"Ben?" she called to him out loud.

Ben's heart sank. He recognized what he thought might be Jonathan's lifeless body.

No! he thought silently. Getting closer to the blurred object, he fixed his eyes on what looked like a child's foot still in its shoe. It barely peeked above the waterline.

Ben gasped hard. His heart skipped a beat. He rushed toward the water fearing he already knew it was Jonathan.

Nancy heard a splash. She turned and watched Ben boldly wade in fully clothed while she ran closer and closer to the river.

Tears welled up in her eyes. Fearing the worst, she darted toward Ben.

Once Ben had completely freed Jonathan's physical body from the branches, he instinctively swooped his arms under Jonathan's legs and neck. Looking at his young friend's face, Ben felt momentary relief seeing the boy. He looked so peaceful.

Ben hoped that death had been kind and instantaneous to the little guy. Nobody this size deserves to unnecessarily suffer. No wonder he wasn't answering our calls thought Ben as he laid Jonathan's pale, blue, still body onto the ground.

By now Nancy was standing on the shore. In spirit form, Jonathan moved close to his physical body.

Nancy shrieked seeing her unconscious grandson. "No!" she innately cupped her mouth and nose in horror. Then she intuitively knelt down and said, "What can I do?"

"Do you know how to do CPR?"

"Yes!"

"Then breathe for him."

Nancy resisted the urge to grab Jonathan's cold, wet body, and simply hold him to her chest. Instead, she waited for Ben to temporarily stop doing chest compressions. When he did, she pinched Jonathan's nose, tilted his head back and gently lifted his chin. Then, she sealed her mouth completely over Jonathan's mouth and breathed.

Suddenly, Jonathan was feeling drawn back into his body. A beautiful angel came and stood by Jonathan.

"It's not your time yet." said the angel to Jonathan.

"It's not my time to do what?" asked Jonathan of the heavenly visitor.

"It's not time for you to return home yet. There's still work for you to do. So, you'll be going back into your physical body for a little while longer."

"How? I thought I was dead!"

"Well, you were. But it's been arranged for you to help your Grandma and Grandpa and some other people learn some important lessons. You'll be helping a lot of people if you choose to come back. And, you get to see how strong you are, too, if you do decide to take on this new mission."

"But how can I be strong? I'm dead!"

"God sees that it is wisest for you to come back here for a little while. That's why things happened the way they did. You know how you and Joey were saving everybody last year from that ferocious gorilla Ooga Booga?"

"But that was just make believe…" said Jonathan's spirit to the angel.

"Sometimes adults need to see the great power in using their imagination for good."

"What does that mean?"

Jonathan and the angel continued to talk as Ben and Nancy worked rhythmically together. When Nancy breathed into Jonathan's lungs raising his chest with air, Ben stopped the chest compressions. They felt hopeful they could bring him back to life.

Church members started gathering around Ben, Nancy and Jonathan. They started to pray that God would deliver Jonathan.

"You see all these people? They love you. See them closing their eyes and praying? They are praying for YOU."

"For me?"

"Yes. For you. Listen to what all these people are saying. Can you hear their prayers? They are inviting in the Spirit of God to think through them. They are not asking for you to be saved. Do you notice that? They are asking for God to do what is best for you. Can you hear them?"

Jonathan listened to the church members praying. What the angel was saying was true. Nobody was asking for Jonathan to be saved. They were all asking for God's will to be done.

The angel continued speaking. "Sometimes people misunderstand how God works. God's will and desire is for you to be happy. And right now, His will is for your spirit to go back into your physical body for a little while and help your family learn some important lessons. If Joey needed your help, would you help him?"

"Sure. 'cuz Joey's my best friend."

"Well, God is your best friend and he's asking you to help your family. And for just a little while longer, he's asking you to help them in a way that only YOU can help them. Would you be willing to help your Grandma and Grandpa and stay just a little bit longer?"

Jonathan looked at Grandma's sad and worried face. "I want to help Grandma because I love her. She's my best friend." He was quiet for a moment. Then he said, "Yes. I will help her."

"That's a good boy. You are a special fellow. You are truly generous to your grandparents. And when you are good to others, God is very generous to you. I promise."

With the innocent eyes of a child, Jonathan's spirit threw his arms around the neck of the angel. "I know I can do a good job. Grandma and Grandpa have taken good care of me. Now I can help them."

"Your faith in wanting to help others makes you whole. God will send people to help you. There is going to be somebody who will help you a lot. And your Grandma and Grandpa's lives will also be greatly helped because you have chosen selflessly to help them. Do you have any questions before you go back into your body?"

"Will it hurt?"

"It will feel different than right now. There will be many people helping you on this part of your journey. But I will see you again soon."

And then the next thing Jonathan remembered was going back into his physical body.

Only about sixty seconds after Ben dragged Jonathan from the water, paramedics arrived on the scene. Thank goodness the park ranger had acted quickly calling 911 just 30 minutes earlier from his office phone.

"Who can tell me what happened?" asserted a female paramedic to the nameless gathered crowd.

"He went off playing by himself. I think he's been under water for about twenty minutes." said Ben.

"Are you the parent?"

"No, she is," pointing to Nancy who continued doing CPR.

The lady paramedic's nametag said McNeal. McNeal turned her head to Nancy. "Please tell me your name."

"Nancy Wallace."

"And what is your son's name?"

"He's my grandson and his name is Jonathan Wallace."

"How old is he?"

"He's eight."

"Okay. Are you his legal guardian and if so, do we have your permission to treat him?"

"Yes, I'm his legal guardian. And of course, treat him!"

Ben and Nancy stopped doing CPR. They stood up and dusted themselves off as the paramedics lifted Jonathan onto a gurney.

Before continuing CPR, McNeal flashed a light in Jonathan's eyes.

"Pupils non-reactive." she said to the male paramedic whose name tag read Sheridan.

Sheridan put a blood pressure cuff around Jonathan's tiny little arm.

"Systole is 55." Way too low for a child of that age thought Sheridan silently.

Sheridan put a tube down Jonathan's throat and started bagging him. McNeal started an IV in a subclavian line. Ben and Nancy stood by mechanically watching the medical professionals do their thing.

Ben put a consoling arm around Nancy. He noticed that she was breathing shallowly. Tears filled her eyes. "Breathe, Nancy. Help is here."

Nancy calmed herself some while never taking her eyes off Jonathan. She started breathing in a more relaxed way.

The medical professionals spoke to each other in their medical lingo. They couldn't rouse Jonathan to consciousness.

"I'm sorry, but we have to get him out of here now." said McNeal to Nancy.

"But that's my grandson. I've got to be with him."

"I'm sorry, Ma'am. There's no room on the helicopter for you. You'll have to drive up."

"Okay. Of course," unconsciously agreed Nancy. Ben took his arm off of Nancy but continued standing by her. In disbelief, she watched the medics load Jonathan's lifeless body onto the helicopter.

Within minutes of finding him, Jonathan was being airlifted to Children's Hospital.

I've got to be with him thought Nancy as she started heading toward her car.

Ben ran after Nancy and put his hand on her arm. "Do you want me to come with you?"

"No, thanks. There's no telling how long I'm going to be at the hospital."

"How can I help you?"

Nancy stood there with a blank face for a moment. "I...uh..."

"Do you want me to go to your house and wait for Tim?"

"That's a great idea. Tell Tim what happened. Tell him I'm going up to Seattle." Knowing Tim would be told about the accident, off she darted to her car. It would take about an hour to drive north to Seattle. Then, being the polite person that she was, she turned back and yelled to her friends. "Thank you everybody."

"It's okay, Nancy. Go! We'll grab your ice chest and folding chair. We're praying for you and Jonathan." called back one of the parishioners.

Nancy's mind raced as she hustled to her car. She got in, thinking disconnected and trivial thoughts. Do I have a full tank of gas? How fast can I drive without getting a ticket? Is it really necessary for me to deal with those arrogant doctors? Oh, why was this the day that Tim went to visit his brother in Tumwater? Rose, you brat! Why aren't you here helping me? Of all the lousy timing!

Chapter Three
The Drive To An Unwanted Reality

Nancy's heart skipped beats as she drove to Seattle. "That's new... Okay, now settle down and b-r-e-a-t-h-e. Calm yourself." Nancy relaxed her shoulders and shifted her weight in the seat while she drove.

"Goodness, givin' yourself a heart attack won't solve anything. You've gotta pull yourself together. Can you imagine Tim being the sole guardian for Jonathan?"

Her mind quickly flashed to the time Tim had broiled a fish he caught fishing. The fish was unrecognizable as food after cooking it at four hundred and fifty degrees underneath the broiler's flames. It came out looking more like a burnt offering to the fish jerky gods.

The potatoes and carrots Tim had once immersed in water inside a pan on the stovetop now sat shriveled in the bone-dry pot. Only a hint of orange and white kibble looking bits peeked through the scorched remnants.

She shook herself from the cooking flashback with her husband of fifty-two years as she pulled into a convenience store. She got out of her car and walked into the store to buy a bottle of water. After her purchase, she quickly got back into her car and gulped down part of the liquid. She did some deep breathing to calm herself. Then, she prayed.

"God, I know you are watching out for Jonathan. Please bring that peaceful knowing into my heart and mind right now because I really need that. I know I'm supposed to have faith that everything will turn out okay...but I just don't have that at the moment...

An invisible peace floated into Nancy's soul just then. It wrapped itself around her heart, mind and body. She felt like somebody had embraced her with a velvety soft glove that covered her from head to toe. She started to cry with gratitude knowing who that somebody was.

After allowing herself to simply surrender to the Love from Above for a moment, she said, "Well, thank you for that. I love you, God, or the angel who is here with me at this time…I think I better get going up to the hospital now. Thank you. Knowing you are here for me means more than anything. Amen."

Nancy put her hand on the key to start the ignition. Before she turned it, she looked around to see if anybody had seen what just happened. She wasn't really sure what had happened, but she knew she couldn't explain the peace that was now her gentle companion.

After she finished trying to scientifically explain what happened, she started the car and backed out of the parking space. Before she knew it, Nancy was pulling in to Seattle Children's Hospital's parking lot.

Nancy didn't really know how she got to the hospital. It was almost like something subconscious had taken over…like she programmed her car on auto-pilot.

Nancy got out of her car and headed to the Emergency Room. She stopped at the desk, identified herself and asked about Jonathan's whereabouts.

The ER clerk looked at her computer screen and said, "He came in through the Emergency Department. But he's already gone to the pediatric ICU unit. It's down a few halls. Here's a map to find the PICU."

Nancy thanked the woman and looked at the map. But she couldn't think. The clerk might as well have handed Nancy a map to the Bahamas. Things just didn't connect for her in that instance.

"Are you all right?" caringly spoke the clerk.

"Sure, fine…well, no, maybe…could you show me where I am standing on the map and where I need to go?"

Nancy stood there for a moment blankly staring at the map. "Sure."

The secretary took the time to point everything out to Nancy on the paper. "If you get lost, there are signs on the walls pointing the way and of course you can ask someone along the way. We're here to help you."

"Thanks. I think I've got it now."

Nancy wandered off down the hall. *How long has it been since I've eaten? Oh, wait. I just ate at the picnic.* This had been the longest day she could remember since her son David had died in the motorcycle accident. Nancy's only son, Jonathan's father, had only been gone three years. But it seemed like an eternity.

And Phoebe, Jonathan's mother, couldn't take the stress of David's death. Nancy thought Phoebe had literally died of a broken heart. That was two and a half years ago. Nancy already had enough hospital visits to last her a lifetime. And now, here she was, back in another one.

As she continued walking to the PICU, she mumbled to herself. "You're not supposed to outlive your children. It doesn't seem fair. And you're certainly not supposed to outlive your grandchildren."

Nancy realized she had been aimlessly walking, without looking at the map at all.

Her legs seemed to plop her body on a bench located directly across from the Radiology Department's check in counter. A lump started growing in her throat as she focused on the day's events thus far.

I need to keep my wits about me thought Nancy silently. A deep breath seemed to bubble up from within relaxing her shoulders a bit. She continued thinking internally to herself. I handled David's accident. I know somehow God will give me the strength to get through this, too.

She looked down the hallway. Feeling spent, her legs refused to let her body up off the bench.

"Are you all right?" asked the counter clerk looking at Nancy.

"No…" she sighed. "No, I am not all right." Tears started streaming out of control down her face.

The fifty-something clerk stood up from her swiveled desk chair, straightened her dress and silently came and sat with Nancy on the bench for a moment. She compassionately laid her hand on Nancy's forearm. With a loving heart, she listened without interrupting as Nancy courageously poured out her despair.

"My husband and I are Jonathan's guardians. I've already buried my only son and his wife. I hope I don't have to bury Jonathan, too."

Tears empathetically welled-up in the clerk's compassionate blue eyes. For twenty-two years, the clerk witnessed many people cry while gracing that stopping off place. Oh, how some had agonized in hopelessness!

That plastic extruded waiting spot seemed to serve as a place where people permitted themselves to release their grief. Many initially resisted accepting the unwanted news about co-workers, friends and family as they vented their objections. Eventually, after they'd unleashed their woes, then they'd get up and forge ahead. She'd definitely seen lots of grieving people from her clerk's counter.

"I need to get to my grandson. The clerk in the ER said he's in the PICU. Where is that?"

The clerk took a hold of the map Nancy held and showed her the PICU's location. "The PICU is right here." said the clerk pointing out the exact spot. "Do you want someone to go with you?"

"Mary Lou? Do you have the chart from the last patient we just saw?" called the Radiology Department head to the clerk.

"I'll be right there, Mrs. Dublin."

"No, I'll be all right." said Nancy. "I really think I'd rather be alone right now. Thank you kindly though. You've been an angel to listen to me."

"If you'd like someone to go with you, I can easily call a volunteer to escort you to the PICU."

"No, really. I'll be fine. Thanks, Mary Lou, is it?"

"Yes. Mary Lou. If there's something I can do to help you, just let me know."

Nancy smiled weakly and sighed at Mary Lou. Then, Nancy's legs unlocked themselves from sitting and some inner strength lifted her tired frame up.

Jonathan's Grandma made her way to the PICU. But it was difficult for her to focus on anything positive.

Her head would not shut up. Goodness! What's the matter with me? All I can think about is how horrible this is. Snap out of it, Nancy.

She steadied herself as she walked to the PICU nurse's desk. Say something that makes sense, Nancy. You can fall apart later. She demanded quiet from the part of her that dreaded being at the PICU. Shush head!

Nancy finally focused her thoughts on what was really important.... where Jonathan was. She waited a moment for the nurse to finish writing in a chart and to look up at Nancy. Her name tag said Summer.

"Hello. How may I help you?" Summer smiled a smile at Nancy that made her eyes disappear. The nurse's friendly smile made you feel like everything was somehow going to be okay.

"Hello. My name is Nancy Wallace. I am Jonathan Wallace's grandmother and legal guardian. Will you tell me where he is?"

"Yes, of course. But first, since you're his legal guardian, I need to see the documents stating that you are indeed his legal guardian."

"I understand," said Nancy. Being especially conscientious about her responsibility for Jonathan, she always carried a copy of the guardianship paperwork in her purse. That was one thing she learned after the court proceedings for obtaining legal guardianship. Getting through that legal mess after David died was a real education for her and Tim. She always had those blasted court documents with her to prove she was Jonathan's legal guardian in the case of an emergency. And she was glad she had them with her now.

Pulling out the papers and handing them to Summer, Nancy allowed, "You'll probably want to photocopy it. Go ahead." Summer smiled again and disappeared around the corner to the photocopier. She returned in a minute handing Nancy back the originals. "Okay. Please come with me."

"Is Summer your first name or your last name?"

"It's my first name. Please call me Summer."

They walked the short distance to the monitored room where Jonathan lay in bed. Before they entered, Summer said, "Mrs. Wallace?"

"Please call me Nancy."

"Okay. Nancy? The first thing to understand is that everyone going into the PICU is a potential germ spreader. To keep things as clean as possible, all of us first go into this scrub room." Summer acted like a tour guide showing Nancy how to sterilize her hands. Nancy already knew how to dress for an ICU but didn't want to interrupt Summer.

A part of Nancy held her back from wanting to go into the ICU. Hospitals seemed like death's door to her after all she'd been through. She heard Summer talking but wasn't listening. Her mind momentarily pulled her into the abyssal shocking memory of David's one-way visit there.

"Nancy?" Summer touched Nancy's upper arm, which catapulted her back into the present time.

"Nancy? Do you understand it's necessary to put on a disposable mask and gown before you go into Jonathan's room?"

"Understood."

"Okay, in just a bit we will scrub up before going into his room. But first, I'd like to explain some things. He wasn't breathing when he came in on the helicopter."

"Yes, I know. I was there when the paramedics came."

"Oh, all right. So, you understand that he has a tube down his throat to help him breathe. He's hooked up to a machine called a ventilator that breathes for him."

Nancy started to shake and cry feeling flooded with a wave of emotion. "I don't know if I can do this."

"It's okay to feel afraid. This can all seem scary." The two women stood outside Jonathan's room for a moment until Nancy collected herself.

"I don't want Jonathan to see me like this."

Summer patiently waited with Nancy saying nothing for a moment. She handed Nancy one of those really scratchy-feeling tissues so famously found in hospitals.

"I'm okay now."

"It's all right. You're doing fine. It's good to let your feelings out instead of holding them in."

Nancy's mind flashed for an instant to her nurse friend, Rose. *She should be here with me right now!*

"I guess so…"

"Shall I continue?"

"Yes."

"As I said, the ventilator is forcing air into Jonathan's lungs for now. However, we feel hopeful that soon he can breathe on his own. Then we'll disconnect the machine. Do you know what IVs are?"

"Yes."

"Good. He's got two IVs running medicine into him for now. Do you know what a catheter is?"

"Yes."

"All right. He also has a catheter inserted into him so he can void urine into a bag. This can all be temporary."

"I understand."

"I know it's unexpected to see your grandson in the hospital."

"It IS."

"Knowing what you're going to see before you really see it for the first time can make the actual initial visit easier on you."

"Sadly, this is familiar to me. I lost my son and daughter-in-law recently. So, I understand everything I need to do before going into an ICU."

"I see. I'm sorry for your loss." Summer paused for a moment. She started to compassionately put her hand on Nancy's upper arm.

Nancy brusquely pulled her arm away. "Don't. Don't be sympathetic to me. Sympathy kills and will make me cry."

"Okay." answered Summer with a start to Nancy's request. "Well, do you have any questions before you go in and see Jonathan?"

"Can I talk to him? I mean…can he hear me?"

"Well, every case is different. But if you assume that he can hear you, think about saying something soothing to him. I don't know what your past experience in an ICU has been, but it might be possible for Jonathan to hear you, even being in a coma. I know this may sound cold, but I am here to help him get better as quickly as possible. So, if you feel like you're about to do or say something upsetting to him, step out for a moment to regain your composure."

"Yes, that's a good idea. I am here for him, too, not for me."

"Okay, good. Keep saying and doing what helps *him*. Imagine for a moment being in his place. What supportive thing would you want a caring visitor to say to you if you were in that bed? Then, after your visit with him today, outside of his ear shot, get the support you need for yourself. Can you do that?"

"I don't know."

"Well, we have a booklet that explains more about TBI which is an acronym for Traumatic Brain Injury. This is a copy for you if you're interested."

"Goodness, no. I don't want to read anything pertaining to TBI for fear I will completely break down."

"Okay. I can respect your feelings. Maybe you'll be interested later. And, if you are, I can give you information about the pediatric TBI support group. Talking with other TBI caregivers can give you a feeling of hope knowing you're not alone.

Nancy stared blankly at Summer. Then, she seemed to be looking through the nurse.

"This feels like a nightmare that I can't wake up from. Will you go in there with me for a moment?"

"Of course." The two women went into Jonathan's room. First, they both stood at a sink in the scrub room scrubbing their hands with germ-killing medicinal soap. Then, they both put on a disposable mask and gown.

When they entered Jonathan's room, just as Summer had explained, Jonathan had tubes and medicine going into him. His eyes were closed and a ventilator rhythmically raised his chest up and down. Even though Summer had prepared Nancy, she couldn't be prepared emotionally for what she was seeing.

Nancy's internal thoughts wouldn't believe her reality. This can't be happening. Just a few hours ago he was eating a hot dog at the picnic. How am I going to take care of him now?

Nancy turned and walked out into the hall. She felt upset, confused, angry, sad, inconvenienced at it all. Summer dashed after her.

"Nancy?"

"I just need a minute to prepare myself a little better." Nancy wrung her hands and tears started to form in her eyes. She breathed in hard to dissolve the lump in her throat. "Okay, ready."

The two women walked back into Jonathan's room.

"Jonathan?" said Nancy leaning in close on the right side of Jonathan's bed. "It's Grandma." She gently wrapped her hand around his contracted, fisted fingers. Jonathan's eyes remained closed. He couldn't say anything with that ventilator tube in his mouth. But one of the monitors showed a subtle change in his heart rate in response to Grandma's voice.

Summer looked on for a moment and then quietly conveyed to Nancy that she was going back to the nurse's station. "Okay," silently mouthed Nancy even though a part of her wanted Summer to stay. She really wanted someone to save her from facing the reality of it all.

As the nurse disappeared, Nancy quickly felt very alone. She really wanted Tim to be with her to hold her and let her know everything would be okay. But she knew that wasn't going to happen.

Nancy silently blamed herself. I did this. I should have been watching him more closely. You're all I have left of David. Nancy leaned up until she stood straight up alongside his bed.

I'm going to be here a while criticized her mind without others knowing what she thought. She stretched for a moment and then got a chair. She pulled it close to Jonathan's bedside and sat down next to him wanting him to open his eyes or squeeze her hand. But he didn't.

She reached into a bag that was usually with her and brought out some knitting. Grabbing onto the knitting needles, Nancy continued where she left off the last time. You could hear a steady click of the needles.

Knitting delved her into an almost meditative state. She calmed herself with the steady knit purl, knit purl rhythm.

Jonathan would love the acrylic blue and green Seattle Seahawks colored afghan Nancy was knitting for him. It would go nicely with the football team's other memorabilia in Jonathan's collection.

The rhythmic sound of the ventilator confirmed that this whole horrible thing *was* happening…right before Nancy's eyes.

Sitting in her chair, Nancy leaned in closer to Jonathan's face. She spoke as if he could hear and understand her. "Jonathan, you are in a hospital. The doctors and nurses are doing all they can for you. Right now, a machine is helping you breathe. But the nurse, oh, your nurse's name is Summer. Isn't that a pretty name? Goodness, Jonathan. I don't really know what to say. But Summer said that maybe you'll only need the machine to help you breathe for a little while. When you get better, they can take it out. Okay?"

Nothing. Jonathan's body lay still. Nancy studied his face and body looking for some conscious response. But Jonathan's body could have been a statue for all the life it expressed.

Ignoring the sudden and unexpected noisy clatter she heard of people talking in the hallway, Nancy continued studying Jonathan's face. Maybe if I look at him long enough, he'll open his eyes, she thought to herself.

"Excuse me." abruptly said a gowned and masked man standing with another man about ten feet away from Nancy. She continued staring at Jonathan for a moment refusing to let anyone interrupt her.

"I'm Dr. McGill. I'm one of Jonathan's pediatricians."

Nancy leaned back in her chair and cocked her neck toward the doctor. She stood up and walked over to the intruding doctors. "Hello. I'm Jonathan's grandmother and legal guardian."

"Oh, hello. Well, I'm here with Dr. Danville, Jonathan's resident pediatrician."

"Hello."

"Hi. So sorry to meet under these circumstances. Do you have any questions for us?"

"Yes. Can we step out into the hall to talk?"

"Yes, certainly.  But first we'll just recheck Jonathan if that's okay with you."  Nancy partly shrugged and walked back closer to Jonathan's bed.  She stood to the side of Jonathan's bed, watching while the doctors examined her grandson.

Dr. Danville bent down and leaned close to his patient. "Jonathan, I'm Dr. Danville." quietly and gently Dr. Danville spoke into Jonathan's ear.  "You're here in a bed surrounded by people who are taking good care of you."

Jonathan remained still when Dr. Danville spoke to him. After he finished examining Jonathan, he stood back up.  He motioned to Nancy to meet with him and Dr. McGill in the hall. Drs McGill and Danville walked over to the bio-hazard container for dirty gowns to dispose of their gowns and masks.

Before Nancy went out into the hall, she leaned over Jonathan and touched his cheek.  Quietly and gently she said into his ear, "Jonathan, Grandma is going to step out into the hall to talk with the doctors for a minute.  I'll be right back."

Suddenly and unexpectedly Jonathan's legs jerked in the bed.  That surprised Nancy. Grandma felt the hairs stand up on the back of her neck.

"I think he heard me.  He's telling me he knows I'm here."

The doctors saw Jonathan's reaction.  Dr. Danville leaned his head back into the room and said quietly, "Mrs. Wallace, that's probably an unconscious movement."

A gut feeling told her Dr. Danville was wrong.  She started to walk out of the room to the bio-hazard receptacle to dispose of her sterile clothing.  She stopped for a moment and looked back at Jonathan.  I'm sure he was letting me know he wanted me to stay thought Nancy to herself.  Then, she continued on to the receptacle and threw away her mask and gown.

Out in the hall Nancy stood with the two doctors.  Dr. Danville started speaking.  "Well, as you know Jonathan was involved in a near drowning incident earlier today."

As Dr. Danville said 'involved in a near drowning incident earlier today', tears started welling up in Nancy's eyes and began free falling down her face.  A lump of grief twisted up into her throat as she started mentally revisiting the rescue scene at Green River earlier that day.

Drs. Danville and McGill stood silently by for a moment as Nancy regained her composure. Once she calmed herself, she said, "I know about the near drowning. I was there."

Dr. Danville said, "Oh, I see. Well," Dr. Danville swallowed hard before continuing. "Uh, hhhmm. As he was pulled out…"

Nancy was in shock, almost looking through him now. She felt like the more he talked the more he was throwing salt into her wounded heart. She did and yet didn't want to hear anymore. With a strained sigh, she raised a dissatisfied eyebrow.

"I mean, er… medics initiated CPR on the scene. The patient was intubated and required ventilation. A subclavian line was placed. While in the ER, the patient received 50 meq of sodium bicarb. A warming process was begun which increased his temperature to 31.7 and the patient was transferred to the PICU."

"I see that he's on a ventilator." said Nancy.

"Yes." answered Dr. Danville. "We hope that will be temporary. For now, all we can do is keep close watch on him. We are doing what's necessary to help him according to his needs."

"Okay. Do you have any other questions for us?" asked Dr. McGill.

Nancy's tiredness temporarily affected her memory. The three stood there for a moment in an uncomfortable silence.

Dr. McGill broke the silence of the unexpected pregnant pause. "Mrs. Wallace? Any questions?"

A lot of what Dr. Danville just said sounded like "blah, blah, blah doctor-ese" to her. Nancy didn't like visiting a loved one in the hospital again. She felt like the doctors talked in code on purpose, keeping the truth hidden from her.

Nancy silently remember the past to herself. They did that same thing when David and Phoebe were in the hospital. Why did the doctors do that? Did they think they were part of an exclusive club? Did they think Nancy couldn't take the truth? Nancy refused to be excluded from knowledge about Jonathan she might need to help him.

"Did you see him move his legs when I got up to leave?" asked Nancy.

"Yes." answered Dr. Danville.

"I think he heard us! I believe he's in there somewhere."

"Mrs. Wallace," started Dr. Danville, "don't get your hopes up. We don't know if he can hear us or not. That might just be him going through what's called a hypothalamic storm."

"What's that? In English please, I'm not a doctor so speak like you're explaining it to a young child sitting in 3rd grade science class."

Dr. Danville sighed an impatient, exasperated sigh.

"What's that for?" referring to his exasperated sigh. "If this were you sitting here worried what to do to help your child," began Nancy, "would you permit a young, impertinent, inexperienced doctor to arrogantly minimize your concerns?"

Dr. McGill looked at Dr. Danville, waiting for his response. He didn't have a very acceptable one.

"No, Mrs. Wallace, I didn't mean anything by my response. I've been awake for 48 hours now. I'm tired and I'm doing my best to explain to you what's happening."

"That sounds like an excuse to me. If you can't manage your time better than this, I want you off my grandson's case. I expect you to treat him with the respect you'd want to be treated with."

Nancy stood up next to Dr. McGill. She pushed her face up closer so she was sure she was heard. "Dr. McGill, I know what a resident is. That's a student doctor. I don't want any exhausted student doctors tending to Jonathan. Do you hear me? You're getting paid by my insurance company and I expect excellent service. Not some amateur doctor who's too tired to think clearly. And Jonathan better get the best service there is, too. I'm holding you responsible to seeing to it."

"I understand you Mrs. Wallace. You're right… this is a teaching hospital. And residents do get tired. Would you like me to be Jonathan's primary doctor?"

"But, he's my patient, Dr. McGill."

Dr. McGill waited for Nancy to answer.

"Yes. I want this pipsqueak off the case."

"Okay, now Jonathan is my patient. Is that all right with you, Mrs. Wallace?"

"Yes, if you are good at doctoring."

"Well, I do have a lot of years of experience tending to children with TBI and other special needs. But understand that, as I said, this is a teaching hospital and there will be residents tending to Jonathan's needs at times."

"I don't like that residents will be tending to him but I understand I have to let them tend to him sometimes. But not THAT Dr. Danville. If you agree to take him off Jonathan's case, then, I agree to let you be his doctor. Now, will you explain to me in simple terms what hypothalamic storms are?"

"Yes, of course. A hypothalamic storm is essentially the nervous system's stress response gone haywire. It is something that happens in the brain after a moderate to severe brain injury. Agitation or restlessness commonly occurs in this type of patient. It is an activity happening most likely due to Jonathan being without enough oxygen while he was under the water."

"Thanks for explaining that simply." said Nancy standing back a little bit from Dr. McGill's personal space. "What's going to happen to Jonathan? I mean, I know you can't predict the future, but with your experience, what's the most likely scenario for Jonathan's future?"

"Do you want me to sugar coat it or bluntly tell you the truth?"

"If you have some backbone, just tell me the truth. When my son died three years ago, I felt like the doctors had their own club. They talked medical-ese on purpose…like they didn't want me to know the truth. So, if you're going to tell me something, just tell me the truth…in plain English."

Dr. McGill paused a few seconds before he answered. This was the part of his job he regretted having. He saw a mother's pain of loss in Nancy's eyes. What did she expect him to say? If she was looking for hope, she'd come to the wrong place.

"To tell you the truth Mrs. Wallace, people in coma individually and uniquely experience it. He could come out of the coma while we stand here talking or he may never come out. I have no control over it. We just have to wait and see."

"That's what I thought. No backbone."

"Excuse me?"

"You're a coward. Don't patronize me. I asked you to tell me the truth and you give me a politically correct, non-committal response. This is your specialty, right?"

"Yes, but…"

"You've seen how many kids like this?"

"I've lost count."

"More than twenty?"

"Yes, more than…"

"You've specialized in kids in coma for how many years?"

"I've been here for twelve years."

"So, in all that time, how many kids have you seen come out of coma?" Nancy's cheeks were flushed. She seethed with inner rage feeling excluded from the truth when it came to doctors.

"Like I said, it's individualized."

"How many?"

"Only a few."

"That's what I wanted to hear. I just wanted to hear you tell me. Don't worry. I won't sue you if you're wrong and Jonathan happens to be one of the ones who regains consciousness."

Dr. McGill patiently and impersonally ignored Nancy's Jack Webb-esque, 'just the facts' interrogation of him. He knew she had had a hard day.

"So, what do we do to bring him out of coma?"

"Mrs. Wallace, there are no simple answers. We will arrange for various specialists to tend to Jonathan's needs. I know this is all very upsetting. If this were my child, I would be feeling upset, too."

Nancy stood there silently waiting to hear anything of use from      Dr. McGill. He explained in detail what tests had been ordered, which pleasantly surprised Nancy. David's and Phoebe's doctors never did that. Maybe Dr. McGill was different from the rest. Had she acted too hastily?

"You're the first doctor who's ever shown me test results, explained what they meant and described what tests are yet to come. And you told me in English. Thank you for that. Goodness this is stressful!"

Dr. McGill smiled weakly at Nancy. "If that were my child in there, and I was a plumber or a business executive, I'd want to know in simple terms my child's status. I like to consider my patient's families as part of a team working for the good of my patient."

"Well, so far, you are walking your talk. Thank you, Dr. McGill. You're a breath of fresh air when it comes to doctors."

Dr. McGill shrugged his shoulders.

"So, where do we go from here?"

"More of the same. We continue the round-the-clock care for Jonathan. When something changes, we might change what we're doing. If what we're doing seems to be working, we keep doing what we're already doing. For now, he looks like he's reached a plateau."

"Plateau?"

"He's somewhat stabilized."

"When you say 'stabilized' do you mean he's going to be this way for the rest of his life?!" Nancy's voice ended with a shudder.

"Just for a moment, consider Jonathan's brain like it's a computer. Do you know how a computer works?"

"Sort of."

"Well, let's compare a computer to a human brain. A computer has the equivalent of a human brain in it. The computer brain is called a CPU or central processing unit. If it's working well, the computer functions well. If something causes it to malfunction, that's called a crash. When a computer crashes, usually you need to get a new computer. Or, pay to have it fixed by replacing a lot of components. Understand?"

"Yes."

"Imagine that Jonathan's brain is like a computer, because it is. It's had a disk crash. His CPU experienced major damage. That means probably little is internally functioning or communicating the way it did before the accident."

"I see."

"But in the case of a human brain, we can't do a brain transplant. We rely on the body's ability to heal."

Nancy bit her lip and contorted her mouth into a grimace as she continued listening to Dr. McGill.

"To tell you the truth, Mrs. Wallace, we doctors don't really heal anybody. The body heals itself and we use drugs and different therapies to facilitate the body repairing itself. The human is amazingly restorative. And, he's a child. Typically, kids bounce back better and faster than the rate an adult does. Additionally, the water might have been cold enough to help minimize some damage."

"But you don't have a real picture yet because…"

"Because right now he's healing. Body parts, cells, brain sections and virtually everything within are swollen and inflamed. His neurochemical balance is temporarily in shock mode. And all that takes time to equalize."

Nancy searched Dr. McGill's face for more information. But she couldn't find any.

"So, what you're really saying is this might be as good as it gets for Jonathan."

"Yes, that's what I'm saying. This might be as good as it gets."

Nancy said, "But that's only from your medical perspective. There might be something else out there, a complimentary answer from one of those alternative practitioners."

"I wouldn't put much stock in anything that has to do with wishful thinking. If it sounds too good to be true, it probably is. Let's just wait and see what happens over the next week. I may get a better idea of how to proceed after that."

"Dr. McGill, I put a lot of stock in my relationship with God. So, I'm expecting a miracle.

"I hope you get one, Mrs. Wallace…for Jonathan's sake."

"Until next Thursday then." said Nancy.

"Yes, no later than next Thursday I will know more." Dr. McGill smiled a forced smile as he and Nancy parted ways for the day. Dr. McGill turned and walked down the hall to check in on another patient.

Nancy went back into Jonathan's room. She was hoping for Jonathan to suddenly sit up on his bed and leap to the floor with a huge smile on his face and say, "Surprise, Grandma. I was just joking."

But Nancy knew this nightmare was real. She was fully awake. Sitting back down by Jonathan's bedside, briefly recalling Dr. McGill's 'no-faith in miracles' opinion, Nancy started to imagine Jonathan's future. His discouraging remarks only offered a bleak picture with him in bed for the rest of his life being tethered to a machine and IV's. This was NOT the life Nancy really wanted for her grandchild.

No! That is just my mind going faithless. I know that God is here in the midst of this. I have faith. I believe that God is here right now with Jonathan. If I have faith that God is taking care of Jonathan, I have no worries. Wait a minute…am I worrying? No, I don't think so. Nancy stopped her mind's endless, pointless, desperate chattering. She started to pray. Silently praying helped comfort her.

Dear God,

I feel worried at this moment. When I worry, I am telling myself to believe and have faith in my fears and worries instead of having faith in your continuous love, peace and serenity which is also here.

I know that if I worry, I show my lack of faith in your presence. Please forgive me worrying. I'm working on this. I know that you are always here with me and Jonathan showing me how to make a change for the good.

I trust you, God. I am developing my skill of having faith instead of worrying.

Thank you for giving me worry situations. When I start to worry, I know to visualize the solution as I prefer things to be…which is seeing myself with you embracing me and steadying me back into your ever-present peace. When I use my inner images of peace, instead of worry, you show me I'm on the faith track instead of the worry track.

I know you are here with me. I know everything is already all right. I love you, God. Thank you. Amen.

Chapter Four
Living Through the Unstoppable Nightmare

Waking up right next to Jonathan's bed in the hospital room sleeping chair, Nancy looked over at her grandson. After hours and a long night being awakened suddenly and unexpectedly by his crying jags, five continuous hours of sleep felt heavenly to her.

What time is it anyway? Wondered Nancy to herself. She lifted her body partway up and leaned on her right arm. She swung her left arm over and looked at her watch through blurry eyes. Four o'clock.

"Ugh!" she plopped back down in the chair looking at the ceiling.

She closed her eyes only to recall the haunting memory of the last crying jag.

"Shhhhhh… it's okay, Jonathan. Grandma's here." quieted Nancy as her grandson's back arched and his body rumbled and shook. It had been the same scene repeatedly.

When it all started, Jonathan went through a seizure of sorts. His body mechanically acting out some macabre script only he lived from within.

It's a wonder he's still all together. He looks like he's imploding. Nancy put her hands on his body to keep him in bed when he shook violently.

Is he going to wrestle himself onto the floor? She wondered watching until the seizure finished its course once again.

In disbelief she internally talked to herself as she watched the horror begin again. There he goes again. I can tell when it's coming to the end. He looks like he's reliving the drowning all over. Then, he cocks his neck back. His mouth forms a circle with his lips and he looks like he's trying to take one last breath. Oh, my poor baby! If only you can hang on one more time. Then, as he successfully rode the storm out again, his exhausted body relaxed back into a more restful pose.

Day in and day out, with a seemingly indiscriminate schedule, he'd go through this routine. And Grandma had been there without Tim for every one of them. They seemed to occur more often at night.

Nancy grabbed her heart and began to cry silently. Tears pooled in her eyes and quietly overflowed down her cheeks.

She lamented to herself. I feel so alone right now. God, please bring peace to my heart and quietness to Jonathan's mind so we can both rest.

Nancy opened her eyes for a moment to come back to the current time. She looked at Jonathan who for the moment, lay quietly sleeping. This had been a better night compared to the previous two.

Grandma turned her head away from looking at Jonathan. This caregiver's eyes burned with tiredness so she closed them. Nancy felt herself melting back into the chair. Her shoulders ached. Holding Jonathan down during his seizures were starting to take a toll on her.

Before she could consciously focus on any more stressful scenes, sleep embraced her once again. It mercifully rescued her for the time being from this unwanted waking nightmare. Then, Tim appeared.

Dressed in sterile garb, Tim barely walked into Jonathan's room. Pastor Jenkins accompanied him at Tim's invitation. The two had met at the hospital exchanging the latest news about Jonathan's condition.

Tim silently walked in behind Nancy who sat in a chair on the right side of Jonathan's bed. Finally, Tim stammered out some words. "Oh, Dear, Lord." His feet suddenly felt like heavy cement blocks. He never did handle unexpected bad news well. Pastor Jenkins stood off to the side for a bit.

A lump formed in Tim's throat. Nancy got up from the chair and walked over to Tim, throwing her arms around his neck. She didn't know that the masked man near the wall was Pastor Jenkins yet.

Tim snugged his arms around Nancy's waist. They both stood there for a moment, lost in a tragic, silent sob.

"I'm so sorry, Nan. I got here as soon as I could." quietly confessed Tim barely audible into Nancy's ear. "This is my fault.

I should have been there. It would have never happened if I had just been there."

After the two stood there a moment entwined in grief, Nancy broke the embrace. "Let's go out into the hall for a moment." Then she darted a glance at the man standing off to the side. "Who's this?" she said to Tim.

"It's Pastor Jenkins." he said identifying himself. "Nancy we've all been praying for Jonathan."

"Pastor Jenkins, it's so kind of you to come all the way up here."

"Well, I came up to visit Jonathan and George Delco over at Harborview. He had a stroke."

"Oh, that's terrible. How is Rebecca holding up?"

"As good as always. They've been married forty-five years and are each other's strength."

"Yes, they are. Please tell them we'll pray for a quick recovery for George." offered Nancy.

"Yes. A speedy recovery." chimed in Tim.

"I'm sure they'll appreciate that."

Tim gently grabbed Nancy's hand. It felt so soft like it usually did.

Together the three adults moved their sorrow away from Jonathan's immediate presence into a world of their own in the hall.

"I'm just going to stay for a moment Tim and Nancy. I wanted to let you know we are all praying for you and your family. If there's anything your church family can do for you, please let us know."

"Well, Pastor, I'm going home every night to feed the dog. So, I'll pass on any news."

"That's good, Tim. Just know that our hearts are with you. Call for any reason. Do you mind if I go in and see Jonathan?"

"Summer, his nurse, is tending to his needs right now. Would you mind making it another time?"

"Certainly. I understand. I'll keep checking with Tim to see what's best."

"Just call ahead. We don't know from one minute to the next how things will be." recommended Nancy.

"Okay. I understand. I'll just be off to Harborview now. I'll call Tim later."

"Thanks, Pastor. We appreciate you coming." announced Nancy. She hugged him goodbye. Tim shook his hand goodbye and Nancy and Tim were left alone to each other.

Tim leaned up against the wall outside Jonathan's room. Nancy cuddled into Tim's loving hug. She fit into Tim's arms like a custom-made, comfortable pair of gloves fits on your hands. Nancy let the tears flow knowing Tim's quiet compassion would help ground her in some form of peace. Tim stood there and absorbed her sorrow like a sponge while silently letting tears fall like autumn leaves from his own face.

They stood there for a moment more before Nancy shared Dr. McGill's news. Tim quietly listened without interrupting. After fifty plus years of marriage, he knew Nancy was not looking for him to cure her sadness right now. There was nothing he could say to do that anyway.

Instead, Nancy simply needed to be heard by someone she knew genuinely cared about her. Just by listening Tim knew she would be better equipped to work through her sadness on her own terms.

After hearing the shocking news from Nancy, he acted on an intuitive nudge to go in and get a closer look at Jonathan. Nancy stayed out in the hall, leaning a bit into the room.

She watched as Tim approached his grandson lying in the bed with medical paraphernalia tentacled to him. He moved over to the right side of Jonathan's bed and sat in the chair. "Jonathan, Buddy, it's Grandpa. I've got some great news. As soon as you get better, we're gonna go on a fishing trip to Alaska. Won't that be something? So just rest for now and get ready for our trip." Okay?"

With that said, Tim could no longer hold back his sadness. "I'll be back. Gotta go talk to Grandma right now."

Spontaneously, Jonathan started crying. But it was more like the cry of a desperate, wounded animal. Eerily bizarre the noise sounded like a combination of a sob, garbled speech and a screeching barn owl. Tim didn't know what to do when Jonathan unexpectedly cried in such a strange manner.

He got up and backed out of the room, nearly running into Nancy who still stood watching by the door. Tim turned around and somewhat hurriedly moved out of the room. Out in the hall, he leaned up against the wall and pulled down his mask. "I'm so, so sorry, Nan." Consumed with grief, he silently stood and stared down at the floor.

After a minute he unconsciously blurted, "Death does come in threes. First David, then Phoebe and now Jonathan. This is too much. It's just too much."

"Jonathan is still alive. What are you talking about?!?" gasped Nancy.

Grieving and in shock about the unexpected, unwanted event thrust upon him, Tim instantly regretted speaking. "You're right. I'm sorry. That was a stupid thing to say."

"Summer, Jonathan's nurse, suggested we only say encouraging things to Jonathan. I think that's a good idea. It will keep our spirits up. What do you think?"

Tim thought about that for a minute. Engulfed in his self-created guilt about feeling responsible for Jonathan's drowning, he struggled to feel uplifted at the moment. He looked blankly at Nancy. He couldn't presently speak.

"Does he do that on a regular basis?"

"Yes. Doctors are medicating him. It helps some but sometimes he spontaneously gets hung up in these crying jags. It's awful."

"Does he know he's doing that? I mean is he in pain or is he trying to communicate with us?"

"I don't know. I just get through it the best I can when it happens."

"What do you do?"

"I stroke his hair if that seems to help him. I stand up and get out of the way of medical staff when it's real bad. I shift my weight on one foot as I stand against the wall waiting for it to end. I cry. I've been doing a lot of deep breathing and praying. I dunno…just stare motionless time in the face and wait for it all to wind down…"

Tim wanted to run away. This all seemed so surreal. "I need to be alone right now. I've got to think about what to do."

Nancy instantly felt abandoned. She had taken the brunt of this unbelievable incident and now Tim said he needed to be alone? What was he thinking? Couldn't he understand that Nancy needed him right now?

She sighed an accepting yet frustrated sigh. In past times when Tim felt overwhelmed, she knew being alone helped him clear his mind. So, though she didn't like it, she accepted that waiting for about forty- five minutes or so he'd be back. And when he returned, he could be there for her.

So, she put aside her need to be held and supported for the moment. "There's probably a waiting area somewhere close. Maybe you could ask a nurse to help you find it."

In that moment, Tim loved her more than he could say. He was a sensitive, quiet, peaceful man. And she was a spiritual, wise, loving woman who understood him better than any other person on earth. She was and always would be his best friend. He gently embraced her hand, pulling her close into his body.

He stroked her hair for a few seconds as she snuggled into his body. She liked Tim's gentle caress in her time of need. It released the anxiety out of her. After a moment, she lifted her head up. He gave her rose petal soft lips a quick kiss, like longtime friends and married couples do. "I've gotta go."

Tim released the rest of his cuddle from his best friend. He started out down a hall to find a place to be alone with his thoughts to rejuvenate himself.

Her best friend off in search of internal strength, Nancy walked back into Jonathan's room. Feeling rumblings from her stomach, she realized it had been five hours since she had last eaten. Satisfying her body's nutritional needs at the moment would have to wait. That seemed a lesser priority compared to what her grandson was experiencing. But it was getting later and later.

The Seattle sky began to darken. Tim had gone home for the night and Nancy found herself once again about to doze off in the chair alongside Jonathan's bed. Nothing had changed as far as Jonathan's condition. All she could do right now was get through one more day.

Nancy lay there in the chair looking up at the ceiling. Ambient light reflected from the hall into the room. She could make out shadow images on the ceiling. One image looked strangely like a giraffe drinking from a water glass. Another one seemed like a cloud wearing eyeglasses. And another one reminded her of the tattoo Rose got in the middle of her back.

"Oh, Rose. You are such a hoot!"

Nancy smiled as she recalled the time her best friend Rose suggested they both get tattoos. "Come on, it will be fun. I've always wanted to do a sister thing with you."

"Yes, but I'm not really your sister."

"You're as close to a sister as I'll ever have."

"I have no desire to get a tattoo. I'll go with you to a tattoo parlor if you'd like, I mean if that's what you really want to do, but I don't want one."

"But Nance, it'll make a great story we can tell our grandkids!"

Rose was that way, adventurous in a way that Nancy could never be. How Rose ever talked Nancy into getting a tattoo she would never understand. She shook her head chuckling at the image of Rose laying on her stomach as the tattoo artist needled away a beautiful rose on her friend's back. Rose seemed to have a high pain threshold in contrast to Nancy's squirming and moaning through the event.

"You've got to hold still, Nancy." Reminded the tattoo artist as he worked on Nancy's right buttocks cheek.

"But it hurts!"

"You're doing great, Kiddo. Just gut it out. You're almost done." said Rose wanting to cheer her friend on through the experience.

But the truth was that Nancy couldn't get past letting the tattoo artist complete the tattoo outline. So, she had let the pain of the needle cut the session short.

"Well, it's a cute black outline of Elmo. But it would look cuter if he was colored in red."

"Nope, that's it. I've subjected myself to enough pain. What was I thinking when I listened to you? You're a bad influence on me!"

Rose smiled a devilish smile to her friend. Nancy shot a glance back at her as she pulled her pants up over her smarting new artwork.

Then, she remembered Rose throwing her arm around Nancy's neck and drawing her close. She kissed her on the cheek and said, "Now you are my tattoo sister. I LOVE it!"

Nancy smiled and fell asleep enjoying the irreverent memory of being at the tattoo parlor with Rose. When she awoke, she tasted sour grossness in her mouth and felt grungy. Yearning for the familiar surroundings of her own habitat she longed to take a shower at home. Each time as she showered, there was that Elmo tattoo on her right hip. It made her chuckle connecting with something familiar and fun and momentarily escaping the insanity of the surreal with Jonathan's situation.

Nancy stretched her arms and stood up from the chair. She looked over at her grandson crumpled up in his bed. "Oh, Rose. I wish you were with me here right now to help me through this all!" She looked at her beloved grandson wanting the catastrophe all to be over.

Minutes morphed into hours and hours stretched into days. Soon, Nancy had been by Jonathan's side for a solid week. Luckily, Tim came up almost every day to be with his family. Jonathan's crying jags had continued to upset them both.

The two had been sitting in Jonathan's room for a couple of hours. Grandma would fluff up her grandson's pillow. She'd talk in low, gentle tones to him letting him know she was there. It was more of an intense whisper. Intuitively, she would do what seemed comforting to him.

It was eleven in the morning. Summer appeared in a cheery pink uniform. "Good morning everyone." She strolled over to Jonathan's bed. "And top of the morning to you my wonderful boy!" engaged Summer at she leaned down near

Jonathan's ear. Speaking in a quiet, soothing voice, Jonathan's body offered no response to her presence. The bright pediatric angel went about checking Jonathan's vitals. Then, she asked Grandma and Grandpa to step out for a few minutes.

"I'm going to give Jonathan a quick cleaning up. Would you like to get up for a bit and stretch your legs?"

The tedium of being unable to improve things for his grandson caused Tim to start feeling antsy. He stood up from the hard, plastic chair he'd been sitting in.

"Nan, I'm going into the waiting room. I'll just be around the corner. Did you see where I put my ball cap? I know I had it when I came in here. I thought I put it with my coat but it's not there."

Nancy glared at him. It was her pet peeve. He rarely put things in the same place twice. As he got older, his habit of misplacing things seemed to be getting worse. It was annoying when he rummaged through her things at home looking for his stuff.

"No. I haven't seen your ball cap. Maybe you left it in the waiting room the last time you were in there." she suggested while rolling her eyes in disbelief. "I'm going for a short walk in the hall while Summer does her thing with Jonathan. I'll walk out with you."

Tim stretched his sixty-three-year old tendons, ligaments and bones as he silently watched Summer tending to his grandson. As he stood there stretching, he triggered an old memory of when he had barely turned nineteen. He'd never forget his 1944 birthday as a World War II, US Army infantry bullet-stopper.

He remembered lying silently on his belly in tall grass. Sweat poured down his cheeks. His helmet seemed to keep the Philippines heat in. He could barely feel the weight of the fifty-pound pack strapped to his back. His buddies lay nearby, all hiding as Japanese soldiers marched by unaware of Tim's squad hidden in plain sight.

While lying there in the grass, feeling petrified, his focus wandered for a moment on him and Nancy in high school. Marrying his childhood sweetheart had been a dream come true for this GI. His flashback threw him back into a memory of them sitting on a porch swing at his folk's house. They were holding hands. He felt so excited when Nancy sat near him, he could barely breathe. *Pay attention!* he thought to himself. But his mind wandered to that long-ago memory when he was feeling afraid and out of control.

Tim barely breathed hidden in the tall grass. He prayed that God would keep him safe. I have faith God is with me. I have faith God is with me at all times. He kept focusing on and silently repeating this simple prayer.

In the memory, he was catapulted back in time when he recalled one of his buddies suddenly tapping Tim on his helmet whispering, "Let's go." Tim looked up to see the threat had passed. He and his buddies had made it. His faith had carried him through what seemed like an impossible moment. Tim breathed a deeper breath as he got to his feet and moved along with the men to finish their mission.

Coming back to the reality of being at the hospital, this moment's mission for Tim was to focus on his strong faith in God. Though it felt like another impossible "tall grass in the Philippines" type of mission, Tim needed to trust that God knew what He was doing.

When Tim's faith momentarily wavered, he started feeling helpless. He felt hopeless when he thought he was responsible for fixing what wasn't supposed to be fixed. A Divine comforting voice suddenly filled Tim's mind with, "Have faith. Trust God." It silenced Worry who was trying to scare Tim into believing an inaccurate, opinionated, human way of seeing things.

Restoring his faithful outlook by believing the Comforter within, Tim let God bring triumph in the moment. Tim's faith continued to be his trustworthy companion getting him through this impossible time for Jonathan.

Tim stared off looking at nothing. Nancy poked him in the arm shaking his endless stare into space.

"Tim?" wondered Nancy.

"Tim? You here?"

"Yes…kind of." he mechanically responded while turning and facing her.

"You said you were going into the waiting room. I'm going for a walk in the hall. Let's go."

"You okay here alone?"

"I'm not alone. Summer's here. Remember?"

"Oh, yeah."

Tim smiled and reached his left hand up to Nancy's right cheek. He stroked it gently and looked tenderly into Nancy's beautiful eyes. "I don't know how you tirelessly stand vigil over Jonathan. You are a miracle."

"Yes, you do know. It's called love." answered Nancy, leaving his admiring compliment unaddressed.

Tim had the kind of eyes that disappeared when he smiled a genuine, deep smile. At that moment, his face swallowed his eyes up into his face. He leaned down and kissed Nancy's forehead. He felt mentally tired. The tedious routine of coming to the hospital and being unable to improve things exasperated him.

"I'd feel better if I could fix this." he whispered into Nancy's ear as they both walked out of Jonathan's room.

"I know." she whispered back. "For now, let's trust God and see what He has in mind for our boy. It will always be in Jonathan's best interest whatever it is."

Nancy's faith that God would take care of everything boggled Tim's mind. Lord, please give me the strong, unwavering faith Nancy has that things will work out right for Jonathan. Please, Lord, grant me patience, but give it to me right now! Tim smiled at the oxymoron of his last thought. As he moseyed his creaky, aging body out of Jonathan's room toward the door, he looked for oncoming pedestrian traffic in the hall. There being none, he moved closer to the waiting room like he had done several times before. Nancy walked off into the hall for a bit.

Tim sat down in the waiting room and looked at the TV. Nancy sauntered off to be in a different setting for a bit. She had complete confidence in Summer caring for Jonathan. But then, eventually she tired of strolling the hall and returned to Jonathan's

PICU room. A part of her felt grateful he was in a single room. Another part regretted having to be there at all.

Eventually the hours unwound the day as they did every day. Tim drove home to feed Fredly and Nancy spent the night by Jonathan's side. Oh, if only God would bring some type of miracle. It was long overdue in Nancy's mind.

"Hi, Sweetheart." suddenly announced Tim as he walked into Jonathan's room. "Another day down and we're still here."

Nancy's husband did his best to sound upbeat. Actually, he dreaded another day of this hospital. He wanted to complain. But unlike many men who might have wanted to leave everything to somebody else, he did his best to stick with everything.

He'd tired long ago of reading old magazines in the waiting room, pacing, getting up and down from the hospital bedside chair, going to the cafeteria and looking for new ways to pass the time entertaining himself.

Tim leaned down to Nancy who sat in a chair near Jonathan's bed. He temporarily pulled down his mask and tenderly kissed her lips. Then, he pulled the mask back up over his mouth and nose as he brought his body up straight.

"Say, you're really moving along on that afghan."

"Yes. This has been a great opportunity to get this made for him."

"And how's my favorite fisherman?" Tim joked as he moved closer to Jonathan's face. He stroked Jonathan's hair gently expecting his grandson to smile in an appropriate response. But that didn't happen. Jonathan stayed motionless except for his breathing. "I'm glad they were able to remove the ventilator. I think this means he's getting better, doesn't it Hon?"

"It is a part of his healing. I asked the doctor when they came in last night. It is a sign of his natural healthiness."

Tim smiled but Nancy couldn't see it under the mask. He thought it was dumb to have to get fully dressed in a mask and sterile gown. But for now, that's what the doctors wanted for some reason. He felt hopeful that Jonathan might recover more, but he kept that to himself. He wanted to keep doing as Summer suggested. Speak in encouraging terms around Jonathan.

As Tim moved away from Jonathan, he turned toward Nancy casually mentioning, "Uh, Ben Michaels says hello. And so does Pastor Jenkins."

"Oh, when did you see them?"

"Well, the Pastor calls regular on the phone. He wants to come up and see Jonathan."

"I just don't know Tim. I appreciate the Pastor wanting to come up here but I feel uncomfortable having him here. I think I might break down in front of him."

"I'll tell him. He just wants us to know he's here for us if we need him."

"Tell him thank you but maybe later. I'm all frumpy looking. I want to be at my best when the Pastor is here."

Tim frowned. "He doesn't care about your frumpiness…"

"Oh, I know. It's me that does. But tell him I'll let him know when I want him to come up. And you said Ben said hello? When did you see Ben?"

"Well, yesterday when I went home, I stopped at the grocery store for some things. Ben was shopping, too, and he asked me how things were. I told him Jonathan was…he was…" Tim stopped himself. He wanted to say something cheerful, especially in front of Jonathan.

Nancy had an expectant look on her face, waiting to hear Tim finish his words. "Jonathan was what?"

"He was as awesome as ever, strong, healing quickly."

Nancy smiled a knowing smile. She realized that Tim had almost spoken words he would have regretted later. Words that might have scared Jonathan. But it can be human nature to blurt out an idea without first thinking about its effect on others. "And what did Ben say to that?"

"He said to tell Jonathan that he's looking forward to the day that the three of us, Ben, Jonathan and I, can go fishing again. He wants me to remind Jonathan that we are the Three Musket Balls, looking to get rolling on the river again soon."

"The Three Musket Balls?"

"Yeah. That's what we called ourselves one time when we went out fishing. Ben was joking that the Three Musketeers name was already taken. So, he suggested the Three Musket Balls could be our name because we have such a ball together fishing."

Nancy chuckled out loud. "That's just dumb."

"Works for us…"

"It's good to hear you laugh."

"Yes. It feels good to laugh. Well, what else did Ben say?"

"Oh, that was pretty much all except to say hi to you. Then, I asked him over to dinner. So, I cooked dinner for us."

"YOU cooked dinner for you and Ben?"

"Yeah."

"YOU?!"

"Yeah!"

"What did you have? Sandwiches and iced tea?"

"Well, um, er, yeah."

"That's not cooking!"

"Well, it is to me. It's the best kind of cooking. I don't burn anything that way."

Again, Nancy shook her head and laughed. It felt good to talk about something other than Jonathan's state of affairs. Then, Jonathan unexpectedly launched into one of his crying jags.

The medical staff came into his room responding to the alarms that had once again been set off. Before the staff came in and took over, Nancy touched Jonathan's cheeks and soothed him like only a mother can do, talking in low, gentle encouraging words.

"Mr. and Mrs. Wallace, please leave the room." blurted Summer as she and the other medical professionals came in to tend to Jonathan. Though they knew the staff meant well, Grandma and Grandpa simply moved out of the way.

Tim was already standing back trying to stay out of the way. He felt frozen with terror imagining what his grandson was going through. In an instant, Nancy stood up from her chair and joined Tim. He grabbed her hand and together they stood helplessly watching their child contort his body uncontrollably.

Soon Jonathan stopped crying and was quiet again. The staff continued tending to his needs.

Nancy felt upset at being unable to stop the suffering. She squeezed Tim's hand and motioned for them to go out in the hall.

"Tim, I really need to get away. I've been here every day for three weeks." divulged Nancy to Tim as they both stood by Jonathan's bedside. Nancy took Tim by the arm and pulled him closer to the door, father away from Jonathan's earshot.

"Get away? You mean you want to go to the waiting room for a while?"

"I mean I need to go home for a day or two."

"Home?"

"Yes, home."

"And leave me here alone with Jonathan?"

"You won't be alone. There's an entire hospital staff here."

"That's going to be hard for me. What if something happens to him?"

"Tim, are you telling me you can't be here for him? And me?" Nancy knew Tim felt helpless when Jonathan spontaneously cried out in horror. She did, too. But she expected Tim to support her. If she ignored her own basic need to take care of herself, she might get sick. So, even though Tim felt nervous about being alone with Jonathan for a short time, she insisted on his help.

Jonathan's grandpa turned and peeked into the doorway of Jonathan's room at his contorted-looking grandchild lying in the hospital bed. "I don't know if I can do this by myself. Sorry, but that's just the truth."

"Jonathan's not *my* grandson. He's OUR grandson. You are not just my husband. You are Jonathan's Grandpa, too. We are here for each other no matter how tough the situation. Isn't that what you always say?"

Tim silently turned and looked at Nancy, then back at Jonathan. "I'm afraid I might hurt him doing this all by myself. I'm no doctor."

A part of him felt like an incompetent dolt. He'd just admitted that he needed help caring for his young loved one. He felt terrified to look weak to his family. What good was he to himself or Jonathan if he couldn't do the job right?

His wife had just asked him to throw himself to the wolves without having the training to do the job well. He dreaded getting involved in a situation where he might further disappoint Nancy and Jonathan. That thought was more than Tim could bear. He was already racked with guilt over Jonathan's accident.

In all the things he'd been through, World War II, David and Phoebe's death, life...Nancy had been his support. At that moment, he'd realized how much she had been his strength. And now, he was expecting more of her? Was that really fair? If the roles were reversed, would he ask her to do a job without the resources to do it right?

Nancy's husband stood pondering his wife's request for a respite. He looked like a deer caught in the headlights of an oncoming, spontaneously unexpected appearing car.

"Tim? Can we count on you?"

With some trepidation in his voice he responded with, "This is so unexpected. I feel unprepared. Isn't there someplace I can get more training before I take this on?"

"Training?!?!" incredulously retorted Nancy with a slight chuckle.

"Tim, it's all OJT as you would say. There is no training for this. It's all on the job training. You're already trained. We've been doing this for weeks."

There was no way Nancy would stop her relentlessness about needing some respite from this emotionally draining situation. Tim was healthy. He had no other commitments, except for seeing Phil on Sundays. And this was Tuesday. It was time to step up. He finally responded with, "What do you need me to do?"

"Just keep doing what you've been doing. Only, instead of going into the waiting room so often, stay by Jonathan's side more. Remember, the nurses regularly come in and check on him. And he is plugged into monitors. They can see what's happening from the nurses' station. It will be okay. You can do this Tim."

Tim gulped hard. "When do you want me to do it?"

"I want to go home tonight. I really need a sanity check."

"Tonight?!?! But I'm not prepared. I don't even have a change of clothes."

"Well, you can turn your underwear inside out. You know, like you did when you were in the Army."

"But this isn't 1944. And I don't *have* to do that!"

"Tim, please?"

Nancy had snapped. All this time sitting there watching Jonathan was just too much for her. A tear ran down her cheek. That tear told Tim she was in need of a serious scenery change.

"Okay. Sure. It's just one night, right?"

"Maybe more. All I know is that I've got to get away today."

Time stood still for a few moments as Tim stayed there in the midst of this unexpected news. Tim never did well when it came to hearing spontaneously delivered bad news. He could relate to what his wife was feeling though. He found the situation impossible so much so he was glad he got to drive up and back each day. His reprieve from the tense situation came every day on a regular basis. It was only fair that she be able to rely on Tim.

"Okay. I'll find a way to make it work for me. It'll be hard but I'll find a way."

"For Jonathan, Tim. For Jonathan."

"That's what I meant."

Nancy knew that Tim wanted to help Jonathan. She knew he loved him. All the time Tim spent with Jonathan taking him fishing, going on camping trips with Ben and Jonathan. Taking him to Cub Scout meetings. Tim being alone with Jonathan would be a good experience for all three of the family members.

Chapter Five
Grandpa's Growth Opportunity

Night fell softly in the hospital room. It had only been three hours since Nancy left but Tim felt lonely without her there. The retired tree cutter stiffly stood up and stretched after sitting so long in a chair by Jonathan's beside. Feeling afraid and wanting to stay encouraged he gave himself a silent pep talk. I can do this. If Nan can do it, I can do it. This is nothing harder than figuring out the correct retreat path. Once I know my escape route, I'm good.

Nancy's husband wanted a change of scenery. He took off his sterile gown and walked into the waiting room.

He thought silently to himself it's good to take that gown and mask off. Tim sat down and thumbed through a magazine. At this late hour, nearly ten o'clock, nobody else was in the waiting room.

"Guess I'll see what's on the news. Let's see what's on KOMO."

Jonathan's aged caregiver clicked the remote to channel four. Just as fast as he had put his finger on the number four, he said beneath his breath, "KOMO…sounds like coma." Internally complaining he said Geez. I just can't escape this! God, what are you trying to tell me here?

Grandpa Tim put his finger on the number five and turned to another channel. "Jason Godfrey, age 18, died today in Seattle when his motorcycle collided with a…" click. Tim changed to channel seven.

"Names have yet to be released in the five-car pileup where one child, aged eight, has a serious head injury. The Interstate 5 traffic is…." with that Tim turned off the TV.

"What is it God? What are you trying to tell me?" he pleaded to God aloud.

Jonathan's grandpa closed his eyes for a moment and started to silently pray. I know you're mad at me, God. This is my fault. And now you're making me be responsible by being here alone with Jonathan. I get that. How can you ever forgive me? I can't even forgive myself.

Tim sat silently praying for a few minutes. But it had been a long day.

And he just couldn't take the stress of everything. Before he knew it, he fell asleep. He was snoring so loudly one of the nurses came into the waiting room. She looked at him and then disappeared. In a minute she reappeared with a blanket. Gently, she draped it over him then vanished out the door.

Sleep deeply embraced him. But his snoring sounded like a foghorn from a Puget Sound ferry warning of its presence. Grandpa Tim's neck tilted back further and further. Though he rarely dreamt, Jonathan's beloved fishing buddy started dreaming.

In the dream, he saw himself methodically walking up a sixty-foot tree. Climbing trees was something he'd done for years as a tree feller in the Pacific Northwest. As he climbed, a Husqvarna four fifty chainsaw dangled off his sturdy tree-logging belt.

He scooted and lifted up the webbed safety belt that safely secured him to the tree. Then, simultaneously leaning into and snugging himself closer to the tree, he rhythmically ascended up the tree's trunk. Closer and closer he moved to the tree's pinnacle intending to top it with his saw.

Inching toward the tree's top, he dug his spurs firmly into the tree's bark. His toes stayed safe inside his steel-toed shoes. Once he reached the perfect place at the top, he pulled up his chainsaw. His safety restraint firmly hugging his body close to the tree, he leaned back for a moment against it. Then, he jerked the saw's ripcord to start its motor. It purred like a mighty lion ready to sink its teeth into the tree.

Tim masterfully moved the saw into place. First, he trimmed some branches away. Then, he moved to the tree's trunk. Like a hot knife through melted butter, the tree's top surrendered to the saw's power. "Look out below!" Tim bellowed to those standing down on the earth.

Then, looking downward for an instant, he darted his eyes along an imaginary retreat path and heard his mind silently figure things out. If I were on the ground, that's the path I'd run along to dodge the falling top crashing down right now. Planning an escape route before even starting to fell a tree was simply common practice for him. Retreat paths gave Tim a sense of control and safety for tree cutting.

"Splat!" announced the treetop as it landed on the ground beneath where Tim had just cut. "Well, that part's done. On to the next."

Tim leaned into the tree a bit, loosening his safety harness. He picked up one foot and jammed the spur in a little bit lower on the tree. Then, he did the same thing with his other foot, moving slowly down the tree. The experienced tree feller intuitively knew where to stop and start cutting again.

Unexpectedly, he noticed some kite string stuck in one of the branches near the next section he intended to cut. Seeing the string in his dream triggered a memory of him flying kites with Jonathan at the schoolyard. When he said the word 'Jonathan' he startled himself awake.

Aware of his surroundings once again in the hospital waiting room, he groggily wiped the sleep from his eyes and wondered out loud, "How long have I been asleep?" The clock said 1:07.

The moon streamed in through the waiting room window. The dotted stars backdrop confirmed it was very late at night. "Jonathan!" remembered Tim out loud, jumping up from the waiting room furniture. He left the blanket behind on the chair and rubbed his aching neck as he headed back to Jonathan's room.

"How has Nancy DONE this all this time?" he wondered incredulously. He felt like he needed some WD-40 to oil his creaking joints when he walked.

Tim peeked in the doorway of his grandson's PICU room. He could see the boy motionless in bed sleeping. Seeing Jonathan quiet, he moseyed over to the nurse's station to talk with Summer. He asked, "How's he doing?"

"The same. Not much changes with him. He moved his legs a little. That's about it. Where's Mrs. Wallace?"

"Well, she needed some time to herself. I'm taking Jonathan duty for now."

"That's good. When the PCG takes care of herself, that's good for the patient."

"PCG?"

"Primary Care Giver." Summer explained.

"Oh, PCG. You have acronyms for everything, don't cha?"

Summer smiled. "I guess we do."

"All this waiting is kinda draining. I never thought that sitting all day long in the same place could be so tiring."

"Yes, it can be. That's why it's a good idea to get up and walk around throughout your day if you're going to be here for a long time."

"Yeah. That makes sense." He stood there for a moment without speaking. Then he asked, "Summer, how do you do it? I mean you WORK here with these kids. How do you get through it all the time?"

"Well, I don't get through it. I look at myself as the voice for these kids who have no voice."

"No voice?"

"Yes, it's a feeling really. I keep asking myself how I can help them. It puts the focus on them instead of on me. It's no inconvenience for me to be here. It's a labor of love."

"Labor of love. Yeah. That's a good attitude. How do you do that?"

"Do what?"

"Have that mindset?"

"I think it's about setting a certain expectation. The parents who expect for their children to miraculously get up and suddenly be healthy feel disappointed when nothing big happens. They feel drained and strained hoping for a miracle."

"Uh, huh."

"But I see that the miracle has already happened. If their children are still living, THAT'S the miracle."

The tall, sturdy man stood silently listening and pondering Summer's remark. "Go on."

"Being here is not about what the children can do for me. It's about what I can do for them so they feel comfortable as they heal."

"Yeah. That's good. Sort of meet them on their own terms instead of expecting them to meet me on my terms."

"Exactly. When you expect them to be able to do only what they can do, and celebrate that, it reduces your stress levels."

"Now say that in simpler terms for me?"

"Love them the way they are and feel grateful they are still alive. That way you aren't waiting and expecting something that may never happen. Just accept that this is as well as they are for now, which might be their forever."

"Hmmm. That's the tree stump hinge."

"Tree stump hinge?"

"When you're cutting down a wooden miracle of nature, you cut a wood notch out at the bottom of the tree. It needs to be a certain length and width. Cutting that notch correctly controls where the tree will fall. The tree falls where you want it to fall when you angle that notch just so."

"Okay."

"Jonathan is like a tree that's been cut down using a badly angled tree hinge. Instead of just getting wet, he drowned in the river. That's like a tree landing in the wrong place. Damage was caused because of his inexperienced choices. Now we all have to deal with it. He might never get any better."

"Oh…kay." repeated Summer with a puzzled look on her face. "What does cutting down a tree have to do with improving the quality of life for a seriously ill child?"

"Well, I'm just trying to figure out what I can do to make things better for him."

Summer could hear that he was processing all the details of the accident. He was thinking it over in a way that meant something to him. She smiled and politely remarked, "Precisely." even though she had no clue what he was saying.

"It's my retreat path."

"What's a retreat path?"

"Well, in this case, it's an attitude. But in tree cutting, it's a path you plan out before you cut the tree down. It's an escape route you can safely travel should the falling tree start going in an unexpected place. It's nothing. Never mind. I think I just figured out how to do better with Jonathan. It's just the way things are which might never change."

"Exactly."

An internal voice revealed an epiphany for him. My attitude has been an obstacle to cutting this tree down about Jonathan. I get it now. There's nothing to fix. I just have to work with this the best I can and leave the rest for God to take care of.

Tim squinted one eye a bit while he continued to figure out what was happening. In that moment, his face resembled, Popeye, the infamous cartoon character. Summer stood there smiling at him for a few seconds more and then blurted, "I've got some kids to take care of. Do you need something else?"

"Maybe later. Nice talk."

"Okay then. See you later."

"Uh, I think I'm going to get some hot cocoa. I'll be back up here to see Jonathan."

"Mr. Wallace, we are tending to your grandson. I know this is hard for you. Take all the time you need in the cafeteria. We've got Jonathan." Summer assured him with a kind smile.

Tim sighed and relaxed his shoulders. "Okay. Thanks."

He headed down to the cafeteria for the chocolaty, warm drink and to be alone with his thoughts for a while. As he walked, he felt peaceful focusing on the idea that the staff was tending to his young Never Quits hunter. Grandpa looked forward to the day Jonathan and he would be out at the river looking that old fish square in the eyes again.

After about twenty minutes away from Jonathan, Grandpa started walking back to the PICU. Somehow, he felt a renewed energy surge through his veins. It was good that he let himself trust the staff to tend to Jonathan while he got away from this intense story for a bit.

As he got closer to Jonathan's room, he simply couldn't face being in there yet. So, he leaned up against the white, painted wall just outside of his grandson's hospital room. A million thoughts ran through his mind.

"What's the rest of the night going to be like?" quietly blurted Tim out loud to himself. In the back of his mind he already regretted being on his own with Jonathan.

Tim liked things to be orderly. He liked being in control and feeling prepared for anything. When he wasn't ready for anything, he felt uneasy. Nancy was the one who knew how to feel comfortable dealing with the unexpected. Somehow, she could improvise at the drop of a hat and make a situation work out okay. But that was a struggle for Tim.

His mind silently complained. I wish I hadn't agreed to do this favor for Nan. If anything goes wrong, it won't be my fault. After all, I'm not a woman. What do I know about taking care of Jonathan when he's like this?

Rapidly reviewing the past three weeks, Tim tried to justify leaving Nancy to tend to Jonathan round the clock while he went home at night. He felt terrified to commit to being the main one to stay day in and day out alongside Jonathan. He just didn't have it in him like Nancy did.

He shifted his weight from one foot to the other. He rubbed his head with its thinning, brown hair. Then, he rubbed the back of his neck while still holding the Styrofoam cup in his other hand.

"Why did this have to happen?! It's all messed up." Tim sighed a deep sigh. He felt he could stall no longer. It was time to go back into Jonathan's room.

He threw away his disposable cocoa cup in a nearby garbage can. He walked into Jonathan's room and once more donned the sterile garb. He complained in his mind. I've never washed my hands so much in my life! thought Grandpa while drying his hands.

Well, better get to it he analyzed begrudgingly in his head. And then Grandpa walked in and took his place on the chair positioned right next to Jonathan's bedside.

Grandpa started to talk quietly to himself. "I wish that was me instead of you in that bed Jonathan. I've already lived my life. You? You're just getting started. It's so unfair."

Jonathan lay on his side with his back facing his grandpa. Grandpa leaned over to see if Jonathan was awake. The side of his grandson's face looked clean, like someone had just washed it. Somebody had run a comb through his hair, too. These were all signs confirming that the staff regularly tended to Jonathan.

Grandpa's focus wandered to a time Jonathan was five years old at his first t-ball game. He and Grandma sat in some lawn chairs off on the sidelines of Jonathan's schoolyard. David and Phoebe sat right next to Nancy and Tim. They watched as Jonathan walked up to the tee with a little bit of a swagger.

"That's my boy!" chuckled Tim to David. Grandpa and his son loved watching Jonathan get involved in the sport. Nancy and Phoebe beamed to each other as they watched Jonathan move so self-assuredly.

Jonathan confidently picked up the t-ball bat. The smallest-sized protective helmet, being too big for him, sat a little bit catawampus on his head. As he lifted his arms and the bat back over his right shoulder to hit the ball, the helmet tipped forward over his left eye and ear.

Jonathan put the bat down and adjusted the helmet so he could see again. Then, he picked up the bat. He started the process all over intending to finally hit the ball only to be annoyed by that ill-fitting helmet once more.

So, once again, he put the bat down and readjusted the helmet. He picked up the bat one more time. He very stiltedly tried to balance the helmet on his head as he moved his arms back into bat swinging position. The same thing happened. That confounded helmet looked like it nearly swallowed up Jonathan's head.

"Helmet!" yelled David from the sidelines. "Let go of Jonathan's head!" Onlookers chuckled.

Jonathan put the bat down on the ground. He straightened the helmet on his head and looked at his family sitting on the sidelines. You could tell he really wanted to hit that ball without wearing the helmet.

"Come on, Jonathan. You can hit the ball now." assured the t-ball coach.

Jonathan stood there for a moment, looking first at his family members and then the coach watching. Something was going on in his mind. You could see those little wheels turning.

Then, unexpectedly, Jonathan put his left hand on his helmet, reached out his right hand and picked the ball up off the tee. Then, he threw it into the outfield.

The crowd roared with laughter as Jonathan started running toward first base.

"Go, Jonathan, go!" roared Grandpa, cheering his grandson on.

The coach started running after Jonathan to get him to abide by the t-ball rules but then threw up his arms surrendering to the impossible situation. It was just as well. By that time, the parents and onlookers were all cheering Jonathan on anyway.

Returning to the present time next to Jonathan's bedside, Tim thought about Jonathan's indomitable spirit during that game. He never seemed to give up. When things went unexpectedly, Jonathan had a way of making the best of it. Maybe Jonathan would wake up out of this coma after all. Grandpa was hopeful he might.

While Grandpa sat looking at Jonathan without any notice his grandson made an unintelligible sound. Tim raised an eyebrow, got up from the chair and walked to the other side of the bed. "Jonathan? Can you hear me? It's Grandpa."

With eyes still closed, Jonathan started to thrash a bit in his bed. He started crying a soulful cry. Then, he arched his back, while tilting his neck and head back into an unnatural, cement-like posture.

Grandpa stood up close to Jonathan's bedside. Alarms were going off. Time froze for Grandpa as he stood helplessly by. He was about to go get help but then suddenly found himself inundated by medical staff.

"Mr. Wallace, please step out of the room." Bluntly ordered Michael, a male nurse, who pushed his way past Tim to his young patient. He almost knocked Tim down to get to his seizing casualty. The nurse leaned down and firmly put his hands on Jonathan's curled up legs to help the boy stay in bed.

The medical staff worked on their eight-year-old patient who was starting to purse his lips together. Something Tim had seen his grandson do before.

"What is he doing?!" asked Grandpa incredulously with a tone of disbelief. This occurrence seemed worse than the past episodes he'd witnessed.

"He's having a seizure."

He panicked inside. I caused this. Lord, please forgive me. Jonathan, please forgive me for not being with you to prevent this from happening.

Grandpa backed away further and let the medical staff tend to his grandson. Jennifer, Jonathan's night shift nurse, talked softly to the young thrashing boy. Sometimes the talk was more of an intense, intimate whisper. She bore her forearms down on Jonathan's shoulders while gently stroking the side of his face hoping to calm him.

"Hang on. We're here Jonathan." She spoke in soft tones as his body rode out yet another stormy electrochemical activity.

He incredulously thought to himself. Is this what Nan has been enduring? Why didn't she tell me it gets this bad at night?

Tim watched in horror. The retired tree feller felt completely out of his element. Instinct told him to do something to fix this mess. But what could that something be?

This six-foot four, mountain of a man had confidently, fearlessly and masterfully scampered up and down sixty- and seventy-foot trees. Then, with a pull of a rip cord on his chainsaw, he knocked those trees down in nothing flat. No tree was ever too big to intimidate Tim. But watching something invisible suck the life out of Jonathan's body cut Tim to his core.

He thought to himself. There has to be something I can do to fix this. There just HAS to be. I should be doing something...

He walked closer to Jonathan. Meaning to encourage him, Grandpa blurted out the first thing that popped into his mind. "Come on Boy, just get through this and we'll be out fishing again soon."

Jonathan's seizure episode was now winding down. Michael stood up, letting go of Jonathan's legs, which were no longer violently thrashing about. He walked over and respectfully put his hand on Tim's elbow ushering him out of the room. "Let's step out into the hall."

Tim and Michael left Jonathan's PICU room. Out in the hall, Michael spoke, "Look, Mr. Wallace. We're guys. Guys like to fix things. It's in our blood. It's our nature to want to fix things we see as broken. With Jonathan, there's nothing you can fix here. Do you understand what that means?"

"It means there's nothing I can do to make things better for him."

"Not exactly… It means figuring out how to accept that the best you can do for your grandson right now is to let us help him through the seizures. I know this is frustrating for you. And maybe you even feel afraid for him."

Tim quietly listened to Michael. "Exactly."

"For now, this is as good as things are. So, if you can just find a way to deal with this, just get through it all, things will be better for both of you."

"You mean give up on him?"

"No. I mean right now you'd like to come in and save the day for your grandson. There is nobody to save here. I know that sounds cold and hard but that's just the way things are. Don't expect him to be able to do anything different than what he's currently doing. Though you can't SEE him healing, those seizures and everything you see him doing are part of him healing. And the healing process is exhausting. So, we just need to help him through it all."

"Healing," asked Tim? "What do you mean healing? You call THAT healing? How much more healing can I expect to see?"

"I can't answer that. Nobody knows the answer to that question."

Tim looked deeply into Michael's eyes searching for a different answer. He didn't want to accept what this nurse was saying.

"So, you're saying there is nothing **I** can fix right now. Just let God take care of everything. Is that what you're saying?"

"Well, I guess you could look at it that way. From a nurse's view, I see him as a patient who is healing. Think about your cells when you heal from a cut. You can see things happening at the cut. At a rate pre-set within the body, the cut heals. There's nothing you can do to heal faster except make sure it stays clean. The healing part occurs naturally. That's what's happening now."

Again, Tim thought for a moment about Michael's words. Then he divulged, "So all I can do is get out of the way and let the healing happen? How much better will he get when he heals?"

"Like I said, I don't know how much better he will get. All I know is that he's going through the healing process. All any of us can do is to patiently wait it out. That's the way you fix this for Jonathan right now... patiently wait for him to heal."

"Okay. I got it. That's something I can do. I won't like it, but I'll do it."

"I've got to get back to the nurse's station."

"Okay." accepted Tim with a somber look on his face.

"You're going to get through this, Mr. Wallace."

"I know. It's just going to take time."

"You got it." smiled Michael reassuringly using his best medical professional demeanor. He shook Tim's hand goodbye and walked away toward the nurse's station.

Tim stood out in the hall alone for a minute. Right before witnessing Jonathan's seizure, he could barely keep his eyes open. He was so tired. After all, it was 2:47 in the morning. But now he couldn't close them. Seeing Jonathan seize unnerved him to his very core. He wasn't ready to go back into Jonathan's room just yet. Needing to be alone with his thoughts for a bit, he meandered into the waiting room.

"Nobody's here. They're probably all sleeping which is where I should be. This is so messed up. This whole thing stinks!"

Grandpa started to pace back and forth in the waiting room while talking out loud to himself. Pacing was how he could think while trying to figure things out.

"He's not going to snap out of this. He can't. His brain is gone! This is just like watching David die. That tube down his throat was keeping him alive. He was a vegetable, too. And then the doctor telling me and Nan that David was already dead."

He paced some more.

Tim got stuck in a mental past image of holding Nancy close to him. Phoebe and Jonathan had just told David goodbye. It was horrible and fantastic seeing Phoebe sobbing and clinging to Jonathan in a desperate hug.

Tim stood there trying to absorb Nancy's shock and sobs of inconsolable grief. Nancy had just kissed David goodbye on his forehead for the last time. Then, she nodded her consent to the doctor to turn off the machines keeping David's broken-down body breathing.

She bent up from her only son's bedside with tears streaming down her face and snuggled into Tim's embrace. He was her sanctuary. Now it was Tim's turn to accept to letting David go.

Tim's and the doctor's eyes met with somber intensity. Tim let go of Nancy for a minute and moved to his son. He squeezed his hand. Then, he stroked his tussled hair. Then he fell down on his knees grabbing onto the bed's side rail and cried. That respirator seemed to taunt Tim demanding he hurry up and accept the obvious. The awful machine sound seemed like a slap in the face reminding Tim he had failed to fix David's state.

Nancy, Phoebe and Jonathan all helped Tim get to his feet again. Dr. Garvy and Nurse Julia stood off to the side letting Tim's family tend to him.

Recomposing himself a bit, he returned to standing. He looked at Dr. Garvy and gave a consenting nod. Dr. Garvy nodded to Nurse Julia. She turned the respirator off and David never breathed on his own after that. Tim stood there stuck in the disbelief that his only child was no more. Then, he brought himself back to the waiting room at the children's hospital.

"No more fishing, no more taking him to ball games. Nothing. It's over."

Mileage started accumulating on his shoe's soles. "I can't stand this!"

Exhaustion overtook Tim. That tends to happen to a person at 3:13 in the morning for someone in Tim's situation. "I am not going to live my life this way. I've already lost David and Phoebe. I will not stand by and watch Jonathan slowly die, too. Not by myself. I just can't do it."

Grandpa stopped pacing and walked into Jonathan's room. He stoutly moved over to his Grandson's bedside and started talking in hushed tones. "Buddy, I've given this a lot of thought. I don't want to admit this but I'm a coward. I can't face watching you go through another seizure. I don't know what to do to make things better for you. Grandma can do it, but I can't. Forgive me."

Grandpa leaned over and kissed Jonathan's cheek. Then, he stood up and walked out the door. He hadn't even put on sterile garb before going into the room. Grandpa had a message to deliver to his grandson and he delivered it. Now, he had washed his hands of the entire mess.

As he walked further and further away from Jonathan's room, he justified leaving his grandson to figure things out for himself. "It will be easier this way. I'm just an anchor around his neck. That's gotta be stressful for him. I'm going home."

The closer Tim got to the parking lot, he felt more convinced his decision was the right one for everyone concerned. He got in his truck and turned on the engine.

"I can go down I-5 and be home in a little over an hour. I'll get some coffee. That will keep me awake. I can easily be home by 4:30. What a way to start a Saturday. It'll be good to sleep in my own bed instead of trying to sleep in those uncomfortable hospital chairs."

Tim pushed in the clutch, pulled the stick into reverse, slowly gave it a little gas and backed his truck out of the parking space. He soon found himself out on Interstate five headed home to Wilkeson.

Chapter Six
It's Just Too Much

Sawing logs in a deep sleep, Nancy was startled awake by the familiar sound of Tim's truck. Panicked that something was terribly wrong, she threw on her robe and slippers and went out to greet Tim.

"What's wrong?!? Is Jonathan okay?"

"Is that all you can say? Did it ever occur to you there might be something wrong with me?"

"You? What's wrong with you?" wondered Nancy, yawning and wiping sleep from her eyes. Her disheveled hair made her look like she had just come out of a wind tunnel.

"I couldn't stay there with him. It was just too much for me being there with him."

"What do you mean, you couldn't be there with him?"

"I mean it was just too much. I don't know how you've done it all this time."

"Don't tell me you can't be there with him. Now is the time he needs us."

"Well, some people are cut out for this kind of thing and I'm not one of them."

"So, you're telling me that you can scoot up a hundred-foot tree and cut it down but you can't do this? Sit in a hospital chair tending to your own grandchild?"

"It's easy to climb up and cut down a tree. That's easy for me. It's what men do. It's predictable. I know how to do it. I can cut trees down almost in my sleep. But this, this is too hard. Watching him have seizures in his screwed-up body. I just can't watch that."

"So, you're going to be a fair-weather friend to Jonathan?"

"What do you mean a fair-weather friend?"

"When things are easy everything's all right. But when stuff gets hard, you give up? So, you're quitting on Jonathan?"

"I'm not quitting. I'm recognizing my limits. I'm a coward. I admit it. I can't face it."

"And if that were YOU in that bed, would me giving up on you be okay with you?"

"Well, no…"

"Then why is it okay for YOU to give up on Jonathan?"

"I told you, I'm not giving up. I'm admitting my limits. I just can't be there alone with him!" recounted Tim as he started to sob uncontrollably.

"I've never seen you like this. Something happened. Tell me about it."

"I started remembering the day David died. It was horrible, but you were there with me. You were my strength. I would have never been able to make it without you."

"You never told me that." uttered Nancy, as she moved closer to Tim putting her hand on his forearm.

"And then I remembered the day we got the phone call from Phoebe's mom telling us Phoebe had just dropped dead at the Safeway in Bonney Lake. And then going to her funeral, too. Did you know that I looked at Phoebe like the daughter we never had?"

"Yes, I knew that. I could tell that by the way you looked when you talked with her. Especially when Jonathan was born. I will never forget the look on your face when you held him the first time. You had such love and respect in your eyes for Phoebe. I'm sorry I couldn't have any more children…"

"No, this is not meant as finger pointing about you. I know having David was hard physically on you. It's a miracle you could even have one child. I'm just giving you information here…"

"I understand…" smiled Nancy as she looked affectionately at the love of her life. By now Nancy was wide awake. She didn't know what to do except listen to help her husband get relief from his sorrow. It was like he had been bogged down in grief similar to a drowning person sinking fast in quick sand. And now he was saving himself by talking about his feelings.

"It was all consuming being there without you. Please, don't make me go back there alone. I just can't face it." Tim stood with his head down looking like a guilty little boy who had just gotten his hand slapped for sneaking a cookie from the cookie jar.

Nancy didn't know how to explain it but Tim bearing his soul made her love him all the more. Being a sensitive man was one of the many things she loved about him. Good or bad, his sensitiveness was something she accepted as a part of her beloved, lifelong mate. She put her arms around him and held him to her body, holding him like she did David when he had skinned his knee as a child.

Nancy put her hand on the back of his head as he stood there crying uncontrollably for a minute. Then she said, "It's going to be all right. I'm sorry I accused you of being a fair-weather friend to Jonathan. I'm glad you told me how you were feeling. We will get through this together."

Tim sighed a big sigh. "I'm exhausted. I know I'm a disappointment to you. That's the last thing I wanted to be."

"You're not a disappointment. You're a man filled with grief. And I'm a woman filled with grief. And right now, that's what we share in common. And we ARE going to get through this."

Tim wiped his tears on his shirtsleeve. Nancy raised her eyebrows as he started to wipe his snotty nose on his sleeve. But now was the wrong time to fuss at him about unsanitary behavior. Criticizing him would not make things better. Instead, she simply let it go.

They kissed each other and stood there embraced in exhaustion. Tim said, "Let's get some sleep. From now on, we will go up there together. I'm sorry I left you alone with him all this time. I will not do that again."

There was a lot of good that came out of this, thought Nancy to herself. I see why Tim was the right guy for me. Thank you, God for this man.

Nancy and Tim went to bed. They slept until noon awaking with growling stomachs.

Tim moved his hands up to the back of his head in a cat like stretch after sleeping. "It's so great to sleep in my own bed. We'll go back to the hospital tomorrow. Jonathan is in good hands. We both need to rest. After all, we're not spring chickens you know…"

"Really, Tim? Couldn't you come up with something less cliché than the 'spring chickens' comparison?" replied Nancy with a slight stretch of her own. She had enjoyed feeling comfy and relaxed in her favorite pink shorty pajamas.

"So, you're okay with us taking a breather for the rest of the day?"

"We'll call the hospital and let them know that we need some down time. Though it seems strange to leave him there alone, I know this is meant to be."

Tim leaned over and gave Nancy a quick kiss on her sweet lips. Then he plopped his body back down on the mattress. He felt relieved she agreed to take some time away for herself. "God will take care of him."

"Of that I have no doubt. He's been there every step of the way so far. I know He never leaves us behind." Nancy turned her head toward Tim. "But tomorrow is Sunday. I know you will want to go see Phil. And I think you should."

Tim turned toward his wife. "Nancy, I will not leave you alone with Jonathan. Phil will just have to understand that supporting you is my priority."

"Phil needs you as much as Jonathan and I do. So, I think you should continue to go see your little brother, including for tomorrow's visit."

"But after what I just experienced, I will not leave you alone. I have a much greater appreciation for you being with Jonathan day in and day out. And I want to say I'm sorry. I've been insensitive to your needs. I want to make it up to you."

"I don't see spending time with Jonathan the same way you see it. I will be all right tomorrow going up to be with him. I want you to go see Phil. But I do appreciate you wanting to support me more."

Tim looked deep into Nancy's eyes as he put his hands on her shoulders and drew her closer to him. "Will you really be all right tomorrow completely alone with Jonathan?"

"I really will be fine. I've needed this time away from him to recharge my batteries. But I'm also feeling like something is about to change. It's like we're in a transition. Like when I felt so exhausted at the end of my labor with David. I wanted somebody to take over and deliver him. But I got through it somehow. It feels like that right now."

"Well, I don't really understand but I trust your judgment." Tim sighed a deep sigh. "Okay then. I will go to see Phil tomorrow. But on Monday, I will come up and be with you every day for as long as it takes."

"Thank you. I appreciate you wanting to be there with me. I feel more supported." Nancy leaned over and kissed Tim on his cheek. "You are a good man."

Tim beamed with an 'aw shucks' kind of smile. "You just lay there. I'm going to make you some waffles."

With flashes of the likely scenario of her eating burnt waffles and having to air out the kitchen, she quickly said, "I think I'd like lunch. I'll get up and rustle us up some burgers and fries. You okay with me doing that?"

"Really, I don't mind making waffles. But, if you insist on burgers and fries, I'll concede to whatever makes you happy." And with that Nancy got up and dressed and headed into the kitchen while Tim turned on the TV hoping to find the latest baseball scores. While Nancy busied herself in the kitchen life went on pretty much as usual at the hospital.

Summer came into Jonathan's room at shift change. "Hello, Sunshine. It's gonna be a beautiful day today."

She went over and opened up the blinds. "See? It's sunny outside. Now, let's see. Last night after I got off work, I went to the grocery store. I bought the greatest piece of salmon for dinner."

Jonathan's nurse chattered on about this and that as she checked Jonathan's vitals and checked his feeding tube. Talking to all her comatose and vegetative state patients in detailed conversation she believed they heard her. At times, when she was very close to a patient, she talked more in intense whispers. She felt hopeful that one day one of them would spontaneously answer her.

"My boyfriend, James, cooked the salmon to perfection. After dinner, we went out for a walk at Sand Point Park. I live really close to that park. It was a lovely evening."

Summer, where is Grandma and Grandpa? spoke Jonathan from within himself. If only somebody could hear me!

"Your grandma and grandpa were very tired and went home last night. You know they told me you have a black Labrador dog named Fredly. That's a wonderful name. I bet he's fun to play with."

What's happening, Summer? Where did Grandma and Grandpa go? spoke Jonathan inaudibly wanting to speak out loud but being unable to.

"And your grandpa goes home each night to feed Fredly while Grandma stays here. Grandma went home last night for the first time in three weeks. Wow. She sure does love you and so does your grandpa. But grandpa stayed for a long time last night. Grandma went home to get some rest. But then Grandpa got too tired and he went home, too."

"Ahhhh!" cried Jonathan with a desperate wail. He wrestled his legs in bed.

"I'm here, Jonathan." Consoled Summer. "They'll be back soon."

Chapter Seven
The Transition

Five weeks had passed since Jonathan's accident. Tim had faithfully come up to stay with Nancy and Jonathan except for Sundays when he went to visit with Phil. Being chained to a routine of a hospital visitor's life for five weeks was draining for both Nancy and Tim at best.

Tim looked at the PICU room wall clock. "Twelve o'clock. You wanna grab lunch?"

"Yes. Let's tell Summer we're going to the cafeteria."

Nancy turned her attention to her grandson and spoke. "Jonathan, Grandma and Grandpa are going to go get lunch. We'll be back soon." They both kissed him goodbye. As was common, Jonathan simply lay there mostly unresponsive.

Mr. and Mrs. Wallace walked over to the biohazard trash can and threw away their sterile clothing. Starting down the hall to the elevator, Dr. McGill unexpectedly stopped them.

"Mr. and Mrs. Wallace? Could I talk with you for a minute?"

The gray-haired love of Nancy's life turned and looked at her. Then, the couple turned toward Dr. McGill.

"Let's walk over to this bench for a moment."

Almost in an orchestrated movement, they strolled over to a nearby bench. Nancy and Tim sat down. Dr. McGill stood up and faced them.

"Mr. and Mrs. Wallace, Jonathan has been here for five weeks now. He's breathing on his own and the medications have regulated his seizures."

"So, what are you saying, Dr. McGill?"

"I recommend that Jonathan be admitted into a long-term care facility. There is an excellent establishment in Enumclaw called Home with A Heart. It's just the type of place that can take care of his long-term needs."

"Are you saying there's nothing else you can do for him here?"

"Mrs. Wallace, we've been discussing along these past several weeks that eventually things would balance out for Jonathan…"

"So, you're saying that time has come? That things are 'balanced' as you put it? You're done with Jonathan?"

"Mrs. Wallace, I think you've gotten your miracle already. How he has lived this long with his massive brain damage is a miracle. It's time to take Jonathan home. Just comfort him for as long as you can. If you don't feel qualified to do it yourself, I think Home with A Heart will provide the compassionate medical care he needs."

Nancy and Tim stared with a shocked look at Dr. McGill. The color drained from Nancy's face. They were speechless for a moment.

"No…no…that can't be all that can be done." barely whispered Nancy. Her hands shook slightly as she held her cheeks between them. She silently repeated Dr. McGill's words in her mind wanting to pretend she didn't understand them.

"Is that all you have to say?" queried Tim looking stoically at Dr. McGill. "This is going to be Jonathan's new "normal"?"

"I wish I could say something more encouraging, but no, there is nothing else I have to say. For us here at Children's Hospital, we've done everything we can do."

They knew this day would eventually come but Nancy and Tim cried hearing the news anyway.

Dr. McGill gently put his hand on Nancy's shoulder. "I'm so sorry."

Jonathan's grandparents sat on the bench holding each other's hands.

Dr. McGill finished with, "We'll arrange for transportation to Home with A Heart by ambulance if that sounds like what you'd like to do."

Nancy couldn't think. "Tim and I need to talk about this."

"Sure. Take your time. Were you headed to lunch? If so, go eat. Talk things over. When you're done, you know how to page me from the nurse's station. If you need it, I can assign a social worker to you.    The social worker can help you decide what's best for Jonathan and the two of you."

Dr. McGill answered his beeper. "I'm sorry but I've got to take this. Just page me if you have any questions."   Soon, Dr. McGill was scurrying down the hall and out of sight.

Tim and Nancy were left there immersed in shock and disbelief.

"Our baby's baby." started Nancy as a tear silently trickled down her cheek. "I knew this day would come but it's all too surreal." Nancy cried.

Tim put his arms around his wife and rocked her a bit. In an instant, his mind flashed to a picture of David's and Phoebe's headstones at the graveyard. But telling Nancy where he was stuck in his head would only make things worse. So, he kept it to himself. Then, he suggested, "Come on. Let's go to lunch."

"I'm not hungry anymore."

"Well, I am. You can come and sit with me while I eat."

Nancy and Tim moved in surreal time to the elevator. They got in, pushed the button on the panel and headed toward the cafeteria. "I feel like I'm in a movie at the part where everything prods along in slow motion. It's like I'm a robot. My subconscious mind is moving my body just to keep moving. There's no purpose to my movement but I don't know what else to do."

"I know, I know." consoled Tim in agreement as he gently held Nancy's hand. "But, just like after we saw David die, accepting Jonathan's new normal is different than condoning that we like the idea. We've just accepted it for now." counseled Tim to his wife.   They both stood silently in the elevator as it edged them closer to the floor where the cafeteria was.

They got their food and sat down at a table. Nancy spoke her mind.

"You know, doctors are only humans. I still believe more miracles are meant to happen for Jonathan." Conveyed Nancy as she sat quietly at the hospital cafeteria's dining table.

"Nancy, are you going to eat your pickle?"

"Tim, how can you talk about pickles at a time like this?"

"Well, I'm hungry. And starving myself is not going to change anything. And you know that. So yeah, I didn't like getting the news this way from Dr. McGill, but I've been kind of expecting it. Haven't you?"

"I have and I haven't. Or rather I didn't want to hear that nothing else could be done. I wish Rose was back from her trip to Europe. I really need a girlfriend to talk to."

"It's going to be okay, Nan. Look, here's what I think we should do. I don't think you and I can take care of Jonathan on our own. Would you agree?"

"Agreed."

"Well, then let's ask Dr. McGill if Jonathan can stay here one more day and we'll go check out this place he recommends. I mean he can't just throw us to the wolves."

"Okay. But if I don't like it, we'll look someplace else."

"Okay. Do you want any more of your potato chips?"

"Take them. You want to eat my coffee cup, too?"

"Very funny. I just think that if we've paid for our food it shouldn't go to waste. Let's look at the pluses here."

"Pluses?"

"We might as well accept it. It'll make things easier on ourselves. I don't like knowing they've done all they can do any more than you like it. I'm just accepting that he might need to go someplace else that CAN help him."

Nancy raised an eyebrow begrudgingly and pursed her lips together as Tim continued. "How can you be so cavalier about everything! You are SUCH a guy. This is our baby's baby." She started crying again trying to feel connected to something but she didn't know what.

"Look, Nan. I don't mean to sound insensitive but we've been dealt the hand we have. If we keep thinking about how horrible it is how does that help us or Jonathan? Let's focus on what we can do."

"Like what?" whimpered Nancy as she blew her nose in a tissue and wiped her tears.

"Well," started Tim as he helped wipe Nancy's tears with a crumpled up Little Caesar's Pizza napkin he pulled from his pocket. "We no longer need to take these long rides up to Seattle. Maybe there will be some occupational therapy or something that can help Jonathan at this new place. And, we can sleep in our own bed again."

Nan looked blankly at Tim for a moment. "No more hospital food. I can be cooking from my own kitchen and talk with my friends more. I have missed the girls at church."

"That's it. Like you tell me, positive attitude. It's all going to be okay, somehow, Nan. Whatever we decide, let's focus on how to improve Jonathan's quality of life. Even if the decision is a tough one. It has to be all about him. That means I will be spending time with him on a regimen. Reading to him or talking to him on a regular schedule, like I do with Phil. And you'll do what you do because that all comes naturally to you. Agreed?"

"Agreed."

"I wonder if Jonathan's really aware of his condition?"

"Tim, I think he may be more aware than we give him credit for."

"How so?"

"I don't know. Just a feeling..." trailed Nancy's thought. "I think sometimes when he cries that's his way of communicating with us."

"Communicating with us? Through crying? Nan, I think that's wishful thinking. And I don't think that will improve the quality of his life. Let's just see what happens."

Tim started picking his teeth with a tine from a plastic fork.

"Seriously, Tim? A plastic fork?"

"Well, I have a piece of coleslaw stuck in my teeth."

Nancy rolled her eyes and conveyed, "The toothpicks are near the exit."

"Ah. Then let's go get one for me. This is driving me nuts!"

Nancy and Tim got up from the table to leave the cafeteria. Nancy was silent as she walked.

She disagreed with Tim but kept that opinion to herself. In her heart, she felt like God had something special in store for Jonathan. This whole thing had a reason for happening. But what could it be?  Maybe Jonathan had to go into a coma for a reason to help others.  That didn't really make much sense to Nancy but she knew God only did things to bless his children.  She was interested to find out what that might be.

Tim and Nancy finished their lunch and went back to the PICU floor nurse's station.  They talked their plan over with Dr. McGill.  He agreed to keep Jonathan one more day.  Nancy and Tim went to Enumclaw that afternoon to check out their grandson's possible new residence.

Home with A Heart, a brand-new group home for medically fragile children, invited Tim and Nancy in with open arms.  The engaging environment and friendly staff gave an instant impression of warmth and acceptance.  Any hesitations in the Wallace's mind about the home being the wrong place for Jonathan melted away.  The very next day, Jonathan became a resident of this very caring place.  Much closer geographically to where Grandma and Grandpa lived, they regularly visited their grandson in his new home.

Chapter Eight
Rose Comes Home

"So, what was Europe like?"

"It was wonderful. Exciting! So different from the US." said Rose to her best friend Nancy as the two gals chatted over lunch at Nancy's house.

"Tell me everything."

"Well, I do happen to have about a hundred and fifty pictures here from my trip." beamed Rose as she pulled out envelopes of photographs. "Tammy and I loved Scotland. We did some genealogy work."

"She's SO lucky to have you for her grandmother."

"Yes, yes she is."

The two women chuckled as they poured over pictures and talked about Rose's trip. Rose would point out an interesting site and Nancy would quietly look on with mild envy.

"I'm so glad you're home. I've missed you a lot."

"I missed you too, but not too much. Sorry, the truth hurts. I really did enjoy myself."

Nancy wrinkled up her nose at Rose feigning irritation. Rose smiled back at her friend with love in her eyes that only a childhood friend could know.

"Well, it's getting to be that time."

"It's kind of exciting when you think about it, Nancy."

"I guess it is. I don't really know what to expect. I mean, I've never met a hypnotist."

"I went to a hypnotist to help me get over my fear of needles. Remember when we got those tattoos? How do you think I was able to do that?"

"You? A nurse afraid of needles?"

"What can I say… I don't mind starting IV's and giving shots but when it comes to getting stuck, I used to be absolutely terrified."

"You'll see, Nan. It'll be okay. If this lady is anything like the hypnotist that helped me, you'll be amazed at the power of the mind. It'll open up an entirely new world to you. And who knows, she really might be able to help Jonathan."

"I tell you Rose, I'm desperate. To see Jonathan each day at HWH and be unable to get through to him is awful."

"I know. I've worked with vegetative state patients and it's tough."

"I hope she can at least help him relax."

"Come on. We'll be late for our appointment to meet her." The two ladies put their lunch dishes in the kitchen sink and hopped into Nancy's car. They headed up to Home with a Heart or HWH as they called it anticipating good things ahead for Jonathan. They were about to meet one of the most interesting care providers ever.

Susan, the hypnotist, drove up into Home with A Heart's driveway and parked her powder blue Ford Courier truck. She stepped out into the August sun's hot, melting rays still hesitant about how she could help somebody in vegetative state.

Susan felt insecure about this new client. Think positively, Sue. There's a reason you feel inspired to do this. Just go with it.

Moving at a lively pace through the nursing home's graveled parking lot she continued the one-way argument in her head with God. I mean really, what was this all about?

A few days earlier at church, the pastor told the congregation about a boy named Jonathan. As Susan listened, her intuition nudged her to go see this eight-year-old stranger.

*What am I doing?* she thought. I have no idea how to help a kid who's been resuscitated after drowning and yet I know I'm supposed to be here.

Still walking toward the building and feeling like she was being led by a voice from the great beyond, she felt intrigued to see what might happen with this opportunity. Susan continued her questions to God knowing full well He had called her here on purpose. What that purpose was remained to be seen.

She stopped for a moment about twenty feet from the entry door and looked up at the heavens. "You sure I'm the right person for this job?"

A voice from within patiently answered, "I do know what I've asked you to do."

Fascinated yet hesitant about the opportunity to work with a comatose child, Susan started walking toward the establishment's door again. She dropped her clipboard, bent down and picked it up. She smoothed out her skirt and began heading toward the building.

"You want me to put my reputation on the line you know… These doctors and nurses are going to laugh at me." she said under my breath.

Nothing. No angel appeared in front of her saying with a lilting voice, "Just joking." She felt doomed to be criticized. And who the heck wants to hear criticism? Even though this was 1989, people still scoffed about hypnosis being useful for clinical purposes. That was one of the toughest hurdles hypnotists had to overcome when finding new clients for their hypnotism practice. Those professional medical people still didn't really understand how hypnosis could be beneficially used in a clinical setting.

But she knew God understood what she was capable of doing. And she knew that if He believed Jonathan would be helped by hypnosis, then she would have to just get over herself.

She had originally started her hypnotism practice to help people build academic skills. As a certified clinical hypnotist, people would seek her out to help them feel calm when speaking publicly. Or, they'd want her to coach them using guided imagery and positive self-talk for enhanced test taking or natural stress reduction proficiency. They'd use those skills to relax so they could think clearly and improve their lives in various areas.

And she felt comfortable helping people enhance their scholarly performance and improve their focus and concentration abilities to achieve practical goals. But this… this was really serious stuff. It was completely different than what she had been doing with personal and professional development clients.

She settled down, finally walking into Home with A Heart's back door entrance. Once inside Susan looked for someone to take her to meet Jonathan and his grandmother.

"Hi, Sandra. My name is Susan Fox. I'm here to see Jonathan. His Grandmother, Nancy Wallace and I talked on the phone about my coming." she said to the nurse that greeted her. The nurse's nametag said Sandra Pierson, RN.

She looked into Susan's face with what seemed like condescending disdain. Then, with an arrogant snort asked, "Are you the hypnotist?"

"Yes."

She huffed and shook her head in disbelief. With a smirk on her face she said, "Well, come on. He's upstairs."

"Excuse me, did I say something offensive to you or are you just having a bad day?"

Sandra fumbled to recover from Susan's confident assertiveness. "Bad day I guess."

That went well, she thought privately. Susan shrugged her shoulders indifferently at the nurse's attitude and followed her up the stairs. She had experienced the arrogance of the uneducated "educated professionals" before about her profession. Susan chalked it up to the closed-mindedness of someone afraid to allow something new to be helpful.

She mentally consoled herself as she walked silently thinking, That's okay. I don't really understand what I'm doing here either...

When the nurse and Susan walked into Jonathan's room, two women sat in chairs on either side of one hospital bed. The nurse turned around, warily eyeing Susan, before she walked out without saying a word. "Hi, my name is Susan Fox. I'm looking for Nancy."

Jonathan's grandmother, Nancy, stood up from her chair. "I'm Nancy."

"Hello, Nancy. We talked on the phone. Nice tomeetcha."

"So nice to meet you. This is my friend Rose." Rose got up from her chair and walked over to Susan. They shook each other's hands and finished their introductions. Then, Susan walked over to the only bed in the room. She stood nearby Jonathan speaking in a normal voice tone.

"Hi, Jonathan. My name is Susan. I'm a friend of your grandmother's. It's nice to meet you." Jonathan lay quietly in his bed staring off into the distance.

Nancy looked at Susan for a moment and motioned for them to go out into the hall. Before they walked out Nancy leaned down to Jonathan and said in a quiet, soothing tone," Jonathan, we're going downstairs for a moment. We'll be back in a little bit." He continued laying there motionless. She kissed his cheek and paused for a moment looking lovingly at him before standing up again. Then the adults all left the room.

Nancy, Rose and Susan went down the stairs away from Jonathan's room. They sat down in some chairs in the downstairs conference room. Rose and Nancy sat down next to each other.

Nancy shared more details about the drowning incident that occurred on July 22nd, 1989, a little over one month before Jonathan came to Home with A Heart. As Nancy spoke, she initially choked back tears. Susan listened quietly as Nancy spoke. Tears started streaming down Nancy's face as she relived the drama.

Nancy continued telling Susan about her own son and daughter-in-law dying as well. This woman had been through so much. Susan admired her inner strength as she struggled to keep back her own tears.

"I should have been able to stop the accident. This is all my fault. If I hadn't been relaxing myself, enjoying the company of adults, this wouldn't have happened."

"No, Nancy, you couldn't have stopped the accident. There are things in this world that are simply out of our control." blurted out Rose. "We may not understand why God allows things to happen the way they do but they happen for His reasons none-the-less. Sometimes we might want to blame ourselves so we can try justifying why they happened, but I believe you weren't supposed to stop it."

"That's just dumb, Rose." said Nancy to her long-time friend.

"No, it's not. Here's what I believe. God sometimes puts us in situations we would have never intentionally arranged to get involved in. Those situations give us opportunities to see how strong we really are. For us, I think this accident was one of those situations. And I also think that we all signed on for this before we came to earth."

Nancy sat there silently listening to her dear friend, her mascara running under her eyes. She reached into her purse and pulled out a tissue and blew her nose.

After Nancy wiped her tears, Rose grabbed Nancy's hand and looked deeply into Nancy's blue eyes as her friend continued talking. "You know in your church you go to, you've told me that your pastor has said repeatedly that real life is eternal. If you believe what he says then doesn't that also mean that earth life is temporary?"

"Well, yes, I guess so..."

"Nancy, I've had way too many experiences with dying patients as a Hospice nurse to disregard the truthfulness of what your pastor has told you. But you already know that because I've told you about my patients as they are in their beds talking about seeing their deceased relatives coming for them."

"I know, some of those stories sound too weird to be made up even for you! Goodness!" Nancy and Rose both smiled at each other. It was as if Susan wasn't even sitting right there listening.

Losing your only child is something nobody can understand unless you've experienced it yourself. Susan had no intention of telling Nancy about her only child dying the year before. She felt frozen and breathed shallowly biting her tongue keeping hidden feelings about her personal experience. She wanted to focus on Jonathan. And she thought Rose's words were also meant for her to hear because she had gone through unexplainable spiritual experiences that initially freaked her out a little after her son passed on.

Watching your child's physical body die is nothing you expect and is nothing you can ever be fully prepared for. It's something nobody should have to go through. At least that's what Susan thought. So, she could definitely relate to what Nancy had experienced.

Rose put her arm around Nancy drawing her near to her. Being with Nancy through David and Phoebe's death, Rose had been a monumental help to her friend during the hardest of times. And now here she was buoying up her dear friend once again.

"Are you keeping a journal of your feelings, Nancy?" Susan asked Nancy.

"Why would I want to do that?"

"Just a thought. Being a caregiver is not for sissies. Give yourself credit for the tremendous job you're doing. Keeping a journal might help you to see how strong you really are. And, it can bring to your conscious awareness your deep feelings during this stressful time."

"What do you mean, it can bring to my conscious awareness deep feelings? I know what I'm feeling and I don't want to feel any more feelings. I'm already exhausted trying to think of how to help Jonathan."

Nancy looked deeply into Susan's eyes, guardedly raising an eyebrow as she searched for understanding of her suggestion to keep a journal. She no longer was crying and feeling hopeless after Rose's words of wisdom. Nancy had actually hypnotized herself at that moment but didn't even know it.

Susan refocused the discussion on a topic that excluded Jonathan's story for the moment. "Nancy, I'd like to explain something here. It's a bit of a digression from what we've been discussing, but it will help you in caring for Jonathan. Do you understand how your brain thinks?"

"Not really…"

"I know this might be a bit scientific, but your brain is actually like a computer. Together with thoughts from your mind, which is like computer software, you use your brain to communicate ideas out to your body through four brain parts or quadrants."

"Isn't my mind the same thing as my brain?"

"No, the mind is really an invisible theory. The brain is something physical and real. They work together."

"Why do I want to know about all that?"

"Understanding how your mind and brain think and work with each other can help you understand how to better help Jonathan."

"Go on…"

"For our purposes, when you write your inner thoughts down on paper, you think thoughts from your mind. Then, you use your brain's four quadrants and they actually communicate with each other to process your thoughts. Hearing ideas or seeing them on paper what you are thinking can spontaneously create new ideas. And by creating new ideas, you can let go of subconsciously hidden concepts causing you to feel stressed. It opens your mind up to new possibilities."

"This is kind of confusing."

"You think thoughts from your mind. Your brain sorts your thoughts into four categories, four types of thoughts so you can know how to make well informed decisions about life situations."

"So, you're saying if I write down what I'm feeling, my brain will reveal to me what might invisibly be upsetting to me?"

"Right. And, it can help you discover new ways of knowing what to do for all your life situations. These ideas are often outside of your conscious awareness. And it is a well-known fact that caregivers might forget about taking care of their own basic needs first. And if as a caregiver you get sick, that means you need to be taken care of. And if you need to be taken care of, what will happen to the level of care Jonathan's getting from you?"

"It could go down…" Nancy suddenly looked like a light bulb went off in her head. "I never thought that writing down my feelings in a journal could be good for Jonathan's well-being." Susan could see the wheels turning in Nancy's mind.

"I didn't know that either…" jumped in Rose.

"And, using certain words actually turns on specific brain parts. Intentionally turning on specific brain parts activates selective programs that effectively help stimulate your ability to maintain wellness."

"Hmmm... and this applies to Jonathan, too?"

"It applies to us all." Susan continued. "Look, from birth, your mind and body, working together, have within inner programs designed to keep us well. This mind/body phenomenon work together for our benefit."

"This is getting too scientific for me."

"Okay, I'll say it more simply. Do you have a home computer?"

"Yes, I use it to write letters but that's about all. I'm not too computer smart. Goodness it's just too complicated for me."

"Well, the program in your computer is what's called a software application program. When you think the word "software" think "electrical" and invisible. Your brain and mind have a similar relationship to this arrangement. The mind contains "software" programs called thought patterns. Your brain is like the computer or the "hardware" which is a physical creation."

"I know this is leading somewhere but I don't exactly understand what you mean. What's the significance of all this?"

Rose sat quietly listening to Susan and Nancy. She put her hand up to her chin intrigued by the new understanding of how her brain and mind worked together.

"A man by the name of Ned Herrmann wrote a book called *The Creative Brain*. In this book he reveals his lifelong discoveries about the brain. He learned that the human brain communicates using the equivalent of four living computer software programs. He calls the whole of these four programs a thinking styles phenomenon."

"And somehow this will help you with Jonathan?" wondered Nancy.

"Yes. And by using hypnosis and these four mental processing programs I believe I'll be able to communicate with Jonathan. And I'm hoping he'll consciously respond to the hypnotic suggestions I offer to him." Susan enthusiastically smiled and raised her eyebrows.

"You're really excited about this knowledge, aren't you, Susan?" shared Rose.

"Yes, I am. I've already been using it. My clients are experiencing greatly improved mental thinking performance as they regularly use it."

Nancy and Rose looked at each other. Though they didn't understand how all the pieces could possibly fit together, they saw Susan's enthusiasm and felt hopefully inspired.

"Let's go back in and see Jonathan." Susan suggested.

The women all got up from their chairs and walked back into Jonathan's room. After they got into his room, Nancy, Rose and Susan sat down in some chairs alongside his bed.

In what doctors diagnosed as vegetative state Jonathan offered no conscious response when talked to. At least he didn't seem to consciously respond.

"Little has changed since the accident. He stiffly lays in his bed." explained Nancy.

"I see. Well, let's focus on saying something positive for now." Susan suggested. "Let's pretend that he can hear everything we say and strive to say something encouraging."

"You sound like Summer."

"Who's Summer?"

"She's the nurse from Children's Hospital in Seattle. She thinks Jonathan can hear everything. It's just getting into the habit of remembering that...it's so hard."

"I imagine it is something new." Susan agreed. "I did some reading on vegetative state before I came here today. From one specific book by Dr. Arnold Mindell and some articles I found at the library, I think it is possible that he can hear everything we say. It might be best to focus on doing what Summer suggested, you know, saying positive things when we're around him."

"I'm for that." chimed in Rose.

For about an hour, the three ladies sat quietly by Jonathan's bed. During that sixty minutes or so, inconsistently, Jonathan would spontaneously cry out, wailing. It was eerie.

There was a TV playing softly in the background. Rose alternated between thumbing through a magazine and watching TV. Nancy picked up some knitting to keep her hands busy. Suddenly, Jonathan cried out like an injured animal.

"Doctors can't decide if his cry is due to pain or an unconscious reaction due to brain damage. While he was in the hospital, almost as soon as he'd start to cry, he'd stop." offered Nancy. "Do you think he's trying to communicate?" she said looking at Susan for an answer.

"Good question." agreed Susan who didn't know. "Maybe we should talk about his condition out of his earshot. If he can hear us, that might be upsetting to him to talk as if he's not here." Susan felt uneasy being looked to for answers in a situation in which she had no prior experience.

"Gee, that's right. Goodness. This is all so unsettling." tendered Nancy.

After his crying jag, Jonathan's mouth stayed slightly ajar. He breathed out in what seemed like a haunting, helpless plea for normalcy again. Excess saliva accompanied almost every gasp.

"Nancy, let's step out into the hall a minute. I'd like to ask you a question." said Susan.

The two women got up out of their chairs and walked into the hall out of Jonathan's earshot.

"Do you know why he gasps for breath?" I asked Nancy.

"No, why?"

"That's a good question, Nancy. I wondered if the doctors could tell you why he breathes like that."

"Oh, no. I think it's just the brain damage."

"Okay. Just curious. Well, I'd like to go back in and observe him for just a while longer if that's all right with you. What I'd like to do is focus on what I see him doing now. I'm thinking about how I might help him using hypnosis."

"Do you really think you can help him? I mean I don't really know what hypnosis is and how it can help. Could you explain how you think you can help?"

Rose heard the women quietly talking and joined them out in the hall as Susan started to talk about hypnosis. "I'm a big fan of hypnosis. I went to a hypnotist years ago to get over my fear of needles. It only took one session and my fear vanished."

"I'm glad you had such a helpful experience from it. Nancy, to answer your question hypnosis is actually a normal and natural nervous system phenomenon. Almost anytime we express a strong emotion we've hypnotized ourselves. Without this nervous system action, we would be unable to live."

"Really?"

"Really. Through sensory-oriented hypnotic expressions such as relaxation, laughing, yelling, feeling angry and emotionally expressing ourselves, we change our brain's chemistry balance. When used correctly, hypnosis, which is a mind theory, helps us learn easier and think clearly. Hypnotizing ourselves we access already stored information in our mind's memory banks or we add information in. Each of us innately hypnotizes ourselves several times throughout our day."

"Goodness. I didn't know that."

"For Jonathan, I'm unsure of when he's consciously or unconsciously aware of the outside world. So, what I plan to do is record some soothing ideas on tape suggesting he breathe calmly. I'm looking for a conscious response from him as he hears the hypnotic suggestions on the cassette tape."

"Do you think he's going to do that? Consciously respond?"

"I actually have no clear idea of his abilities right now. As I said on the phone, I've got lots of experience helping people eliminate their nervous public speaking and test-taking fears.

Working with a vegetative state client is new to me. But I think it's worth a shot. And you must think it's worth doing, too, otherwise you wouldn't have agreed to let me work with him."

"I'll be honest with you. When you called me after church that day you heard about the accident and suggested there might be something you could do to reduce his stress, I was desperate to try anything. The doctors have all been so depressing. They say they can't do anything other than what they've already done. Goodness, they've all but given up on him. But I expect a miracle."

"And so do I." agreed Rose.

"I hope God can give you one through hypnosis. Let's go back in the room so I can keep observing Jonathan, okay? Unless you have more questions about hypnosis…"

"No, no more questions for now. Let's go back into his room."

They re-entered Jonathan's room and sat down in the same chairs they had just been occupying before going into the hall to talk. Nothing about Jonathan had really changed. He still looked like a statue in his bed.

Since working with a vegetative state was new to Susan, she figured she'd just fake it till she made it. She continued observing her new client in his hardened pose. It reminded her of seeing her son who was in and out of consciousness in the last days of his life.

For an instant Susan's mind flashed to last year in Jason's room. She recalled the moment just minutes after her twelve-year-old son died at home in his own bed. In the flashback, Susan had just walked into her son's room like she had been doing every ten to fifteen minutes that Father's Day and realized Jason's chest was completely still.

In that moment after she realized she had found Jason's dead body peacefully quieted and no longer suffering, she felt shocky. She stepped around the corner and stood for a moment looking at her husband sitting on the living room couch who sat watching TV. He silently looked over at her.

"I need a time." She stoically said with tears streaming down her face. Feeling cold, she wanted to move her feet, but felt them frozen to the floor. In that moment, she started to shake and then waited for her husband to come to her side.

He looked at her with disbelief and shock knowing what her statement meant. The Hospice nurse had told them that if Jason passed when she wasn't there, somebody should remember to look at the clock for a time of death…for the death certificate.

With almost instant tears in his eyes, he leaped up from the couch and raced to her. They both went in to Jason's bedside. They mechanically re-entered Jason's room. Susan moved to the opposite side of Jason's bed from where Rudy, her husband, moved. They both started to sob uncontrollably knowing he had completed his earth mission.

Practically, attempting to focus on the idea that Jason's spirit was still alive, but that just his physical body had died, proved impossible for his parents. All they could do was stand there and sob.

For Jason, all possibilities for his recovery had been exhausted. He had been born with a rare birth disorder called Marfan's Syndrome. His heart had so many defects in it that heart surgery would have been impossible.

Marfan's Syndrome was something present in Susan's first husband's genetics. Her second husband had adopted her son knowing full well Jason's days were numbered. All they could do was focus on improving his quality of life during his last days. Susan could relate to Nancy's desperate feelings to do something to help Jonathan. What was God telling Susan putting her in a situation again with a tragic story involving a child's very short life? She didn't completely know except that there had to be many blessings in it for her highest divine purpose.

Throughout his short twelve years on earth, Susan had taken Jason to many medical specialists. She knew what losing an only child meant. Maybe that was part of the reason she was here with Jonathan. Susan could empathize with Nancy's plight.

After observing Jonathan for a little while longer, she finally decided to focus on suggesting something to calm Jonathan's breathing. It was something she could do to help Jonathan improve his quality of life. Was she courageous enough to stick with this after what she had just gone through the year before with her own son? She didn't really know.

She shook herself from the memory of Jason's bedside and came back to Jonathan. Focus, Sue... she thought silently to herself.

To her, Jonathan's entire body looked like a marbled mannequin chiseled into a horror-struck pose. As he lay in his bed, he appeared to be spontaneously and unpredictably reliving the moment he drowned in the river. Oh, that poor kid's brain! Susan wondered what images mentally held Jonathan hostage as he lay stretched out on his bed.

As she sat watching him, Jonathan suddenly opened his eyes wide and arched his back. He pressed his lips together looking as though he were struggling to keep his head above water.

His arms and legs though splinted, briefly paddled furiously while lying in the bed. He appeared to be miming what looked like an attempt to get to the water's surface. But almost as soon as the pantomime began, it ended with Jonathan looking like he had surrendered to the moment.

During the actual drowning, Susan thought he must have felt panic-stricken with every body cell screaming for air. She envisioned that only the angels tended to him as the water entombed and then took away his conscious ability to save himself.

She imagined The Angel of Death hovering nearby in the water, greedily wringing his hands as he anticipated stealing Jonathan's life right then and there. But obviously Jonathan's Guardian Angel played a trump card preserving basic life for him. Otherwise, how could he be laying here crumpled into this awkwardly queer looking position in this comfortable hospital bed?

His body stayed arched into this unnatural spastic contraction. Obviously, the brain damage had rearranged his brain's neurology cutting him off from using everyday life functions. No longer privileged to consciously move at will, he relied on caregivers for everything.

Expecting to live forever, as we all commonly do as kids, Susan bet Jonathan thought he was invincible. Who could have ever guessed something like this would happen to him? Certainly not Jonathan.

This was Jonathan's test. What would life be in the near future for him? She didn't really know, but felt intrigued to find out. And felt sure Jonathan wondered what his future held for him, too. After all, God wanted them to meet. Of that she was sure.

Chapter Nine
The Details Make The Difference

After sitting for a while in the chair near Jonathan's bed, Susan asked Nancy to follow her downstairs again. Rose stayed behind with Jonathan by his bed.

Susan took out her notebook and started asking Nancy questions about her grandson.

"Nancy, I'm looking to find out ideas I can use to reduce Jonathan's stress. Reducing stress for him could help improve his quality of life. In my mind, no matter how long he might live, he still deserves to be treated with loving care. I feel sure hypnosis can help in this regard."

"I see."

"When writing hypnosis scripts, a hypnotist creates suggestions meaningful to a client. In working with people, you can help them reduce stress and help them achieve their goals using their own life experiences. Thus, the value in understanding what makes sense to them."

"Okay."

"So, I'm going to ask you a lot of questions about Jonathan. Whatever I can use to help him, I will. Is that all right with you?"

"What do you want to know to help my grandson?"

As Susan spoke with Nancy, and wrote down notes on paper, she kept thinking about Jonathan and what might be important to him.

"What are some of Jonathan's favorite activities to do?"

"He likes playing with typical little boy types of toys. Ones that run on batteries and ones without batteries."

"Like what kind of toys?"

"Dump trucks, steam shovels, toys that dig in the sand and dirt. He likes Transformers, too."

"Those toys that appear in one shape and transform into another?"

"Yes. He has a toy box with several of those transforming toys in it."

"What's his favorite color?"

"Red."

"What are some of his unique attributes? Does he like to help out around the house? Is he a loner? What's his personality like?"

"He has a close relationship with God. He likes to help people. He's very kind."

"I see."

"He's very protective of the weak. He got suspended one time at school for trying to stop a boy from bullying some little girl. Both boys were suspended because White River Elementary School has a zero-tolerance level for violence."

"Uh. huh. I see." Susan wrote quickly as Nancy explained about Jonathan's character.

"Anything else about the activities he likes to do?"

"He likes to play card games."

"Which ones?"

"Crazy Eights, Slap Jack, Uno and especially go fish."

"Sounds like games an eight-year-old would like to play."

"Yes."

"What about favorite holidays?"

"He loves Christmas. He likes the Christmas carols, the toys he gets and the colored lights. He also likes when it snows. He's told me more than once that he loves winter."

"Okay. That's all good to know."

"What about his favorite food?"

"Pizza. He LOVES pizza with pepperoni. He likes peeling them off, trying to twirl them in the air and then catching them in his mouth."

"I think just about every kid loves pizza. Okay, just a couple more questions and we'll be done for now. Does he have a favorite book?"

"Every night, if I would let him, we'd read Green Eggs and Ham. He likes the rhyming in it. I love hearing him laugh so we do read the book a lot."

"Hearing a child laugh is wonderful. I agree."

"What about his favorite number. Does he have one?"

"He likes the number 3. He's got a book he wrote about himself. It was a school project. I can share it with you if you'd like. A lot of this information is in there."

"That would be great. Next time we meet, would you bring it for me to see?"

"Yes."

"Just one more question for now. Does he have a favorite TV show?"

"Duck Tales. He likes all the adventure stories."

"Okay. Great."

"What do these questions have to do with reducing his stress?"

"Well, whether you can identify it or not, I'm guessing both of you are experiencing stress. In situations where people must cope with an instant change in life routine, there's typically stress. And, the thing that greatly helps reduce stress is to reconnect with the familiar."

"I see."

"The one constant in life is change. A lot of us do not like change. In fact, many people inflexibly resist change. It has to do with the way the brain thinks. The brain likes continuous familiarity. When change comes along, the brain has to figure out how to adapt or cope with the change. Some people find change exciting, others find it stressful."

Nancy started to talk low and quiet to me. "I feel guilty about this. You never expect to outlive your children or your grandchildren. If he dies because of my negligence, it's not fair for me to live."

Then, she got quiet. "I tell Jonathan those three magic words "I love you" often. It's important for him to hear it and know it. One thing I've learned about coping with my son and my daughter-in law dying and now this... If I take the time to tell people important to me that I love them, they can hear it when they are still alive. That's important to me."

"And to them. People usually remember how you make them feel. That creates a special bond between us as humans." I offered. "Nancy, remember what Rose said? There is no way you could have known this was going to happen. It was an accident. You're doing the best you can do in a very unexpected situation."

"Say that again?"

"I encourage you to think of this accident as something temporary rather than permanent. Because you can think any thought, think thoughts that cause you to feel peaceful inside. That is a simple way to cope reasonably with this unwanted situation. Instead of tricking your mind into believing nothing can be done to make things better, anticipate and expect that you *can* and *will* find a way to make things better. That's how you improve the quality of your life. And when you feel better about you, you naturally do things to improve the quality of Jonathan's life and the lives of those around you because you approve of you and what you do."

Nancy chewed on what Susan was telling her. Then she uttered, "Do you really believe Jonathan can get better?"

"Yes, Nancy, I believe we can do something to make things better for him. When I heard about Jonathan, I felt inspired to help him somehow. I've already explained what hypnosis is. But, here's a practical, everyday example of it."

"Okay."

"You know when Jonathan was a baby? And he felt upset? What did you instinctively do to help him?"

"I held him in my arms and rocked him."

"And what happened when you did that?"

"He calmed down."

"When you saw that he was calm, what else did you do?"

"I smiled at him and told him what a beautiful baby he was."

"Did you say anything else?"

"Sometimes I'd sing him a lullaby. At other times I told him that everything was going to be all right."

"And so he felt comforted hearing your voice. He trusted you were there to help him, right?"

"Right."

"And did you notice that your focus was on him and what might comfort him rather than on what he could do to please you?"

"I never thought about it that way but I guess so."

"When you spoke slowly, lovingly and gently to him, you were actually stimulating his nervous system in a particular way by telling him a story soothing and acceptable to him. It was a comforting story. That specific way you stimulated his nervous system is called *hypnosis*."

"It is?"

"Yes. As parents, when we suggest ideas to our children, and they believe those concepts, research indicates that we are also hypnotizing them. When we suggest ideas to our kids, we are really telling them a story."

"I see."

"And we are actually using a gift God already provided for us in the nervous system. The same thing happens when we interact with any human. If we speak respectfully to ourselves, we hypnotize ourselves into feeling good about ourselves and the things we do. And, when we speak respectfully to others, they feel good about themselves. It is such a simple gift to share love with each other in this way."

"A gift?"

"Yes, a gift. When we encourage our children and friends, co-workers and family to develop their abilities in a constructive, forward moving way, that's a gift. It's challenging to be a parent because we don't always know what to say to our children in every situation. None of us comes with owner manuals. But if we suggest that our children allow themselves to be drawn toward that which feels constructive, respectful and peaceful, they grow up learning how to trust their own judgment. And, to make good choices."

"That is a gift. Goodness, I didn't know that I was hypnotizing my David or Tim or anyone!"

"It's an innate behavior. We intuitively do it because within our DNA from birth we follow that program. Without being able to hypnotize ourselves, we'd be unable to build our memory banks or access what we've stored in our memories. Learning how to correctly and effectively use hypnosis in an uplifting way with ourselves and our children is the closest thing we have to creating an individualized human operating manual. And each of us can benefit from using it regularly."

"How?"

"Well, I can teach you some stress reduction techniques. But I can also show you how to use your mind to create options you would have never consciously thought of. When you tap into your loving, highly intelligent spirit/mind/body connection, you connect with God. Prayer is a form of hypnosis but most people don't know that."

"Really?"

"Really. And as we focus on praising God for bringing us into situations and in contact with people also interested in peaceful life, He suggests helpful ideas to keep creating those meaningful, respectful relationships. And life is all about relationships. And He does it in a way that makes sense to each of his children in an individualized way."

"So, when I pray, I'm hypnotizing myself."

"Do you feel relaxed when you pray? Do you intentionally focus your thoughts on thinking respectful, calm and loving thoughts before you go before the presence of God?"

"Yes."

"Are those strong emotions you're expressing?"

"Probably. Yes. I guess. I don't really know."

"Well, if you allow me to teach you how to use hypnosis optimistically and in a manner that attracts more peace and simplicity into your life, maybe you'll discover the answers you seek."

"I would like to feel more peaceful right about now in my life."

"The more you know yourself, the more you'll become comfortable seeking for peace in your life."

Nancy looked pensive and quiet for a moment. Susan continued explaining the value of knowing one's true self.

"So, asking all the questions I've asked about things Jonathan likes, I will write him stories using information familiar to him. The parts of his brain that are still working properly will like that. I will write simple hypnotic stories and ideas suggesting ways he can consciously achieve goals…like breathing calmly and relaxing. Doing this, I'll provide a constructive learning model for him just like parents do when we securely encourage our children to excel."

"But I thought that hypnosis was something else."

"Like the work of the devil?"

"Well, yes."

"Unfortunately, Nancy, there is some misinformation circulating about hypnosis. Hypnosis is actually a common yet extraordinary nervous system phenomenon. We really can't completely explain what hypnosis is just as we don't really understand what sleep is. But I can tell you that if each human naturally hypnotizes him or herself on a regular basis several times throughout his or her day, wouldn't it make sense to learn how to effectively use it?"

"Hmmmm…"

"Basically, as I've already briefly shared with you, we do know that almost every time we express a strong emotion, we also create a hypnotic mind state. Many professional hypnotists believe that all hypnosis is self-hypnosis. Just as only you can eat and digest your own food, only you can hypnotize yourself."

"I see."

"Using hypnosis, we add to and access already stored memory information in our mind. According to the way we consciously understand the information stored in our subconscious memory, we make decisions using that information."

"It sounds a little too technical for me to really grasp. Tell me again how hypnosis can help Jonathan?"

"Well, by hearing encouraging ideas, I believe he can improve the quality of his life."

"Which will reduce his stress."

"Yes…that's if he can hear me like I think he can. Think about him right now, the way you currently see him breathing. Would you say he looks like he feels stressed out?"

"Yes."

"Well, I believe that stress can be reduced by using hypnosis even for people in coma or vegetative state. And, I especially believe this now that I've read Dr. Mindell's book."

"When he's not conscious of the world around him, what good does a hypnosis script do him?"

"That's why I'm here. I think he is conscious some of the time. And, the rest of the time he's hypnotized. When his mind is relaxed and open to learning, I think he can be coached to consciously respond."

"How long do you think that will take?"

"I have no idea."

Nancy looked at Susan with hopefulness in her eyes.

"Let's do it. If you can help him stop reliving that terror of being in the water, I'm willing to try."

"You noticed that, too? It's amazing that we see the same thing. I think that's what he's doing, too. Okay. I've got some releases including one for his doctor. And I'd like a copy of his medical records, too, if that's okay with you. After these forms are signed, I'll start working with him."

"That'll be fine. Please, help him. You just might be an answer to my prayers."

"God surely works in mysterious ways. If I'm supposed to be able to help Jonathan, I'm sure a way will be made. Let's go back upstairs."

The women walked back upstairs and into Jonathan's room. Rose greeted them at the door and said, "I'm starting to get a little tired. I'm ready to leave. How about you Nan?"

"Yes, I think we can leave now. Let's let Susan get to work."

We said our goodbyes. Rose walked over to Jonathan's bed and tussled his hair saying, "See ya' later, Champ." Then, she headed toward the doorway.

Nancy went over to Jonathan's bed, leaned down and kissed him on the cheek. "Gramma's going to go home for tonight. She feels very tired. I'll be back tomorrow." She raised up, quickly glanced at Susan and smiled weakly before she walked out of the room. Susan walked over and sat down in a chair at the end of Jonathan's bed.

Nancy and Rose started walking downstairs. Then, something happened in Nancy's mind. She came back into the room with mascara-streaked cheeks.

"I wanted to say goodbye to Jonathan again before I left." she said almost apologetically to Susan. Did she feel guilty about showing her grief over Jonathan's injury? In Susan's mind there was no reason to feel guilty about expressing her sadness wherever it was coming from. Susan had been in the grips of a mother's misplaced guilt feeling responsible for being unable to stop Jason's death.

Nancy leaned over and kissed Jonathan goodbye again. He looked like he was asleep. She whispered into his ear, "I'll be back tomorrow."

She smiled and mouthed 'goodbye' again to Susan and quietly walked out of his room.

Pen in hand, Susan wrote down observations about Jonathan as she watched him sleep. At one point it looked like he opened his eyes and looked at Susan. But she couldn't be sure. Susan started to pray for enlightenment. She hoped later that Saturday afternoon she could come up with a suitable script that would work. Only God would know how to guide her in the right direction. After all, everything she was doing was because God was guiding her. She was merely His servant.

# Chapter Ten
## Coping and Figuring Things Out

"Oh, hey!" smiled Phil as he recognized his brother Tim. Tim walked toward Phil from down the hall at the day room in the nursing home. Phil got up from the chair where he'd been sitting and put his arms around his brother.

"Hi, Phil. How's my younger brother with a full head of gray hair?"

"Huh?"

"Here, let's sit down and watch some TV." smiled Tim as he and his brother sat down on some chairs in front of the day room's TV. As they sat there, they watched a football game with some other men who also resided at the Tumwater, Washington nursing home. After a little while it was half-time.

"Phil, I want to talk with you about something that's really troubling me."

"Huh?" said Phil looking blankly at Tim with a typical Alzheimer's 'the lights are on but nobody's really home' type of look.

"Do you remember who Jonathan is?"

"Is he that boy who helped us paint your porch?"

"Right. He's my grandson and your nephew. Good memory. Do you remember I was telling you he had an accident?"

"That's too bad…"

"I told Nancy that I would do everything I can to help him get better. But my heart's really not in it."

"Huh?"

"Talking about Jonathan my grandson."

"Oh… the one that's hurt…"

"Yes!" brightened up Tim. "You remembered."

"What will you do to help?"

"Well, when he was in the hospital I would go up to Seattle and read to him. But because he's so sick he couldn't answer back. And he still can't answer back. There is a part of me that really feels like it's all a lost cause. Like I'm wasting my time visiting with him."

"Huh?"

Tim knew Phil only had periods of appropriate memory call back. Usually he couldn't understand or recall what Tim was talking about. And coming to visit Phil felt very similar to visiting Jonathan. Even though Phil couldn't really remember from one moment to the next when Tim was with Phil, he was glad he was with his brother.

The two men sat there silently for a moment. Phil turned his attention back to looking at the TV.

After about 30 seconds of silence, Tim suddenly said out loud to Phil, "I think I just have to stop making this be all about me."

Phil turned and looked at Tim and said, "Oohhh! Hi, Tim!" In less than a moment, Phil had forgotten Tim was sitting right next to him. Phil smiled big showing his pleasure at seeing Tim as if Tim had just arrived. He put his arm around Tim and patted him on the shoulder.

Tim shook his head feeling deep sadness at Phil's loss of worldly awareness. "Hi, Phil. How are you doin'?"

After sitting there silently watching the TV for just another minute or two, Phil suddenly stood up and walked out of the day room. Tim got up out of his chair and followed Phil. He watched as Phil walked through a doorway and down a hall that led to his residence room. Phil soon disappeared into his room.

Tim walked down the hall and peeked in Phil's room. His brother had lain down on his bed and went to sleep completely forgetting that Tim was even there.

"I'll just go get some lunch before I go back home." Sometimes Phil just wasn't in a mood to have visitors.

When Tim got home, he read a note from Nancy saying she and Rose were up visiting Jonathan. "I don't know how she does this. She is an amazing woman that just keeps finding a way to stay hopeful. This is all so depressing for me. I think I'll just take a nap." As Tim went to sleep, he didn't care for the moment about what was happening at HWH or with anyone else. He was focused on taking care of himself.

Susan was talking out loud to herself, figuring things out. "Okay, God, the thing that seems obvious to me is to suggest for Jonathan to relax everything inside, to breathe through his nose, to close his mouth, to swallow calmly and just relax. How does that sound to you?"

Nothing. Susan was hoping to hear God's voice from above. She wanted to know exactly how to write this first hypnotic script, but she didn't see any lightning bolts from the sky or hear an angel.

"So, I'm on my own here? And how in the world am I going to know if he hears me? Maybe you could give me a signal if I'm on the right track…"

She kept noodling around ideas for a simple hypnotic script by talking out loud and hoping to hear from God. Did she feel scared she'd look like a crackpot? Yes, but she walked through the fear anyway and just went ahead and wrote the script.

"Okay. I'm gonna guess I've gotta go through a learning curve here. It's going to take trial and error. So, whatever happens this time, I'll just go with it. Everyone has to breathe. Like Dr. Mindell says in his book, look for something obvious to start on. So, I'll start with the breath. I'll just see if I can figure out what parts of his brain are working. At the end of the script, after I suggest for him to breathe calmly, I'll ask him to smile. And if he smiles, then I'll know he heard my other suggestions. I have faith that everything will turn out all right."

She sat down at her computer keyboard and started to type. While she typed, she kept imagining Jonathan smiling. "I hope this kid remembers how to use his face muscles." Finally finishing the first script, Susan recorded the hypnosis story onto a cassette tape. Then she listened to it and decided it was good enough for the first story.

She picked up the phone and dialed Nancy's number.

"Nancy? Hi, this is Susan Fox. I've got this first hypnosis tape for Jonathan ready. What I'd like you to do is to buy an auto reverse tape player. I've recorded this same first script on both sides of the cassette tape. Because I'm unsure when he's consciously aware and when he's not, I figured what we could do is just play the tape continuously out loud so he can hear the hypnotic, stress reduction suggestions. How does that sound to you?"

"Sounds good to me. Going to buy the tape player today. Can you meet me at Jonathan's this afternoon?"

"Sure! What time works for you?"

"Let's say… 2 PM."

"Okey dokey. 2 PM it is."

After she hung up the phone, she thought out loud to herself, "This is gonna be very interesting."

When 2 PM arrived, Susan met Nancy at HWH. Nancy was waiting for Susan in Jonathan's room. Sandra Pierson was in the room taking Jonathan's vital statistics.

"I've plugged in the tape player. I feel very hopeful that something good is gonna come of this, Susan. This is a Sunday I'm gonna get a miracle for Jonathan."

"Here you go…" she said handing the cassette tape to Nancy. She smiled as she popped it into the tape player and depressed the play button. Instantly, you could hear her soothing voice suggesting for Jonathan to breathe calmly.

"I feel hopeful something amazing is going to happen as well." she said grinning back to Nancy as she heard her voice play out loud for everyone to hear.

Nurse Pierson ripped the blood pressure cuff off Jonathan's arm and she finished recording his blood pressure stats. She looked up at Susan after Nancy and Susan both expressed their hopefulness that the tape would help, rolled her eyes and shook her head. Susan didn't care about Sandra's disbelief and faithlessness. She knew that everything was in God's hands anyway. It was meant for Jonathan to experience an improved quality of life as a result of using hypnosis, it would be Him doing it all.

Nancy left strict orders to let the tape play continuously unless Jonathan became agitated. "Sandra? The doctor and I have discussed using hypnosis with Jonathan. He says it's all right for us to use it with him. So please just leave this tape running so Jonathan can hear what Susan is saying on the tape."

"Yes, Mrs. Wallace. I hope that something good happens for Jonathan as a result of using hypnosis as well. But I'm gonna be honest with you, I have my doubts."

"Well, I'd like you to keep those doubts to yourself please because I believe that Jonathan can hear everything that you're saying. I'd like him to hear something positive."

"I understand. You might be right."

Secretly, Susan was happy to hear Nancy admonish Sandra to keep her doubts to herself about hypnosis. She had worked with enough clients to know that hypnosis does work effectively to naturally reduce stress. In fact, it's one of the safest, drugfree ways stress can be reduced in people.

"I'll be talking with you soon, Susan."

"I expect to hear something wonderful, Nancy."

With that both of them smiled and Susan left the nursing home. She went home and took it easy for the rest of that very warm Sunday. Soon, Jonathan started to positively respond to the hypnotic suggestions.

"Angela, it's time for Jonathan's feeding tube to be checked. Why don't you go on upstairs and make sure everything's in order." said Sandra to one of her staff nurses.

"Ugh. It's so hard to get going on Mondays…"

"What's that?"

"Nothing. Going to see Jonathan now." agreed Angela Pearl, another RN who worked at HWH. Angela got up from the chair that was sitting next to Sandra's desk and headed up stairs to Jonathan's room. As supervisor over the nursing staff, Sandra wanted to keep working on the next weeks' work schedule.

"When Mrs. Wallace sees that hypnosis can't possibly help her grandson, we won't have to be bothered by that hypnotist." mumbled Sandra under her breath as she worked on her papers.

When Angela got into Jonathan's room, she looked at his face. He seemed to be sleeping with his eyes closed. In the background, she could hear the hypnotic suggestions continuously playing by Jonathan's bed. She reached over on the bedside table near Jonathan's bed, opened up the drawer, and pulled out a pair of disposable gloves. Standing by his bed, she started to yawn.

"Funny, I didn't feel sleepy until I came into this room. Her voice certainly is soothing…" Angela noticed as she listened to the hypnosis tape playing in the background. With disposable gloves on, she went over and checked Jonathan's feeding tube that was hooked up through his skin and directly into his stomach.

Looks good the nurse confirmed to herself after inspecting the tube.

"You look like you're feeling much calmer, Jonathan." gently remarked Angela to Jonathan as she moved closer to his ear. She stopped for a moment and listened to the tape playing.

"… and when you're ready to let me know you want to learn something else, just give me the smile signal, Jonathan. That's right. When you smile, that's our secret signal just between you and me. When I see you smiling that's when I know you're ready to learn something else."

Angela chuckled as she heard this suggestion on the hypnosis tape. Then she looked over at Jonathan and gasped.

"Oh my gosh… Jonathan, are you smiling?"

She sat down in a chair near Jonathan's bed. "I'll just wait here for a moment and listen to this entire tape. What exactly is this hypnotist suggesting to you?"

Angela eagerly waited to hear the smiling signal suggestion on the tape again. "… and when you're ready to let me know you want to learn something else, just give me the smile signal, Jonathan. That's right. When you smile, that's our secret signal just between you and me. When I see you smiling that's when I know you're ready to learn something else."

This time, she intentionally watched for Jonathan to smile… and he did. "Is that possible? Can you hear me Jonathan?"

She waited for the five-minute tape to go through its entire cycle again. "Come on, Jonathan, you can do this."

"What is taking you so long?" unexpectedly blurted out Sandra as she abruptly and unexpectedly appeared in Jonathan's room.

"Look at Jonathan. Notice anything?"

"Like what?"

"Like notice how he's breathing now."

The two nurses stood there for a moment watching Jonathan while listening to the hypnotic suggestions play in the background. "He's no longer breathing Cheyne-Stokes." observed Sandra.

"Keep watching…" eyed Angela at Sandra. She was waiting for her boss to hear the smile suggestion come up on the tape.

"Did he just smile?"

"Looks like a smile to me."

"That's impossible."

"That's what's taken me so long. I sat here and listened to that hypnotist's tape complete the script more than once. Every time it came to the smiling signal part of the tape, Jonathan smiled."

"I don't believe it."

"Just watch. That smiling signal suggestion is coming up again." said Angela as the two nurses watched Jonathan's face.

"He smiled again. Why that means…"

"He CAN hear us!"

Sandra sat down in a chair by Jonathan's bed and listened to the hypnotic tape play two more cycles. Each time it came to the smiling signal suggestion part of the tape, Jonathan appropriately smiled.

"This is a miracle you know." smiled Angela. "Didn't that hypnotist just bring the tape in yesterday? That's what it says in Jonathan's record anyway."

"Yes. Yesterday. I just don't believe this. In my ten years of working with kids in vegetative state, I've never seen anything like this. I'm gonna call Mrs. Wallace. This will make her day." beamed Sandra.

Sandra got up out of the chair and walked over to the telephone. The Wallace's phone number was written on a paper that was tacked up on the wall. As she dialed the Wallace's phone number, Angela leaned down, smiling and got close to Jonathan's ear. She quietly spoke, "So you really are in there somewhere, aren't you Jonathan?"

Angela could hear Sandra excitedly speaking on the phone to Mrs. Wallace. "Hello? Mrs. Wallace? This is Sandra Pierson from HWH. I've got some good news for you. Jonathan is consciously responding."

"What do you mean he's consciously responding?" Said Nancy who turned to Tim and started waving her hand wildly to him. He was sitting in his favorite easy chair reading the paper.

"It's that hypnosis tape. The nurses don't really like listening to it because it causes them to feel drowsy when they walk into the room. It's hard for them to focus on what they're doing because they feel so relaxed when they hear it. But it's helping Jonathan."

"How can you be sure it's the tape?"

"Well, Angela and I are here in Jonathan's room. Angela was checking Jonathan's feeding tube and sat here for a few minutes listening to this tape. Well, rather than me explain to you over the phone, why don't you come and see for yourself. It's impressive really."

"We'll be there in twenty minutes." excitedly answered Mrs. Wallace as she hung up the phone.

"Tim! That was Sandra from HWH. It's a miracle. Jonathan is consciously responding to Susan's tape."

"What exactly does that mean?"

"I don't know, but will you come with me so that we can see together?"

"Of course. Maybe he will be ready to go fishing again soon."

"I'll be ready in a jiff. First, I've gotta call Rose."

Quickly, Nancy called Rose with the good news. "When you get home from work, I'll have an update for you after I've seen it with my own eyes."

"As soon as I can, I'll come and see it for myself. For now, I'll be waiting for your call."

Nancy hung up the phone and she and Tim drove off to HWH.

Chapter Eleven
The Magic of a Smile

"Hello?" Susan spoke directly into the phone.

"Susan! This is Nancy. Are you busy?"

"Not at the moment. What's up?"

"What I was going to say is whatever you're doing stop and come and see Jonathan."

"What's going on?" fearing something was terribly wrong.

"I'm so excited, I can hardly speak. So, stop what you're doing now, and go and see Jonathan."

"So, you're not gonna say anything other than that?"

"Please… If you can, stop what you're doing right now and come and see Jonathan."

"Are you with him now?"

"Yes. Just please come and see. See you in a few minutes. Bye."

"Okay. I'll be there in a little bit. Bye."

"I wonder what this is all about…"

Susan got into her truck. Within about 20 minutes she was pulling up into the HWH driveway. She got out of the truck and walked up to the back door and walked in.

"Hello Ms. Fox. It's all very exciting isn't it? I was wondering if you would be willing to work with another one of our patients here who's very similar to Jonathan." blurted out Sandra.

"What are you talking about?" said Susan suspiciously eyeing the nurse who had initially greeted her with skepticism.

"Jonathan! Haven't you heard?"

"I'm just on my way up to see him now."

"Well it's astounding and great what has happened. If you haven't seen him yet, I won't spoil the surprise." she said grinning an ear to ear Cheshire cat sort of grin.

Susan looked at her guardedly wondering what awaited her upstairs. She walked into Jonathan's room. Sandra followed her up the stairs.

Nancy and Tim sat in the chairs on opposite sides of Jonathan's bed greeting her with huge smiles on their faces when she arrived. Sandra slipped into the room and stood by the wall. As Susan stood just inside the doorway, she heard her recorded voice still playing out loud on the tape player broadcasting the customized hypnotic suggestions for Jonathan.

"… and when you're ready to let me know you want to learn something else, just give me the smile signal, Jonathan. That's right. When you smile, that's our secret signal just between you and me. When I see you smiling that's when I know you're ready to learn something else."

Just after listeners in the room heard this one suggestion, Jonathan smiled.

"That one part sends chills up and down my spine as I watch my grandson smile, Susan." confessed Nancy with tears in her eyes.

"I've listened to this tape several times in a row now. He only smiles when you ask him to smile. I wouldn't have believed it if I hadn't seen it with my own eyes. This is no coincidence. It's the hypnosis that's doing this." somberly spoke Tim.

"And he's breathing calmly. Look, through his nose with mouth closed, like you've asked him to do. I don't understand how this works, but obviously you do. This IS a miracle." chimed in Nancy.

"What's the next step?" asked Tim.

Susan scratched her head. "Great question!" She nervously laughed a little.

"Well in my mind, I think we should keep working with what seems obvious."

"What seems obvious to you?" pondered Tim.

She studied Jonathan for a moment looking at his curled-up hands. "Tim, would it be all right if I sat in that chair for a bit?"

"Sure." agreed Tim as he got up from his chair and stood up near Jonathan's bed.

Susan leaned close to Jonathan's right ear. She quietly spoke, "Jonathan, this is Susan. I'm going to stroke your right cheek with my fingers. Before I do that, I'd like your permission. If it's all right for me to gently stroke your cheek, I'd like you to let me know by smiling right now."

All eyes were on Jonathan's face. At first, nothing happened. The delay in his response caused Susan to doubt that he could hear her. And then all at once Jonathan smiled.

Nancy put her hand to her mouth with quiet excitement. Tim drew his hand up under his chin and marveled at his grandson consciously responding with a smile. Sandra stood off to the side equally amazed at Jonathan's progress.

"Okay, Jonathan. I'm going to touch your cheek. I'm going to touch your cheek Jonathan. Jonathan, I'm going to touch your cheek. I'd like you to pretend, Jonathan that as I'm touching your cheek, your body feels very relaxed and happy. Jonathan, pretend that as I touch your cheek, you feel calm and relaxed and happy." As Susan touched his cheek, the smile remained for about a minute and then started to fade.

"I have never been so happy to see him smile." remarked Tim.

"Jonathan, I'm going to ask you a question. And I would like you to answer by using your smiling talent. If it's easy for you to smile and use a smile to answer questions, I'd like you to smile again right now. But if it takes a lot of energy for you to smile, I'd like you to just leave your face relaxed."

They all eagerly waited to see a smile. But it didn't come. Instead, nothing happened. Susan got up from the chair and motioned for everyone to follow her out into the hall. Then she offered her best opinion of what had just happened.

"Well, I think we have an answer here. It may be exhausting at the present moment for Jonathan to use a smile as a way to consciously respond. So, I think we should let him sleep. And I think we should do this exercise again later. We're in a learning curve here figuring out how to communicate with Jonathan using his level of ability. Those learning and conscious awareness levels may change from moment to moment depending upon the brain damage and his energy levels. So, if we try to push him, we could cause a relapse in all the progress that he's made. I also think that for now, we should turn the tape off so he can sleep. Let's go back in his room and I'll talk with him and tell him what I think is best for him for right now."

They all gathered back in Jonathan's room. Susan sat down in the chair on the right side of his bed and leaned over and talked quietly to him. It was more of an intensely intimate whisper really. The others stood nearby. "Jonathan," Susan began, "we think you need to sleep now. I'd like to tell you a short story."

Jonathan lay there quietly. Susan felt certain he was listening.

"When I was a little girl, I had a toy bear. My parents put batteries in it and it would beat a toy drum. I loved that bear with the toy drum. And I started to use up a lot of batteries playing with that toy."

Jonathan continued to lie quietly in his bed. He breathed at a deliberate and peaceful rate. Susan spoke very slowly and in a monotone voice. By speaking in a monotone voice Susan knew Jonathan could most easily hypnotize himself. Susan's intention was for him to hypnotize himself into a relaxed state. She believed the more you relax yourself as you are letting your body naturally heal, you facilitate the entire healing process.

"My parents eventually told me to go outside and play with other children. I grew up in a place called Arizona. In Arizona, the weather is very warm a lot of the year. So, going outside and playing in the warm, friendly, clean air helped re-energize me."

Susan continued to use a hypnotic, monotone voice for Jonathan to use as a model to relax himself. She knew that as he naturally relaxed himself, he also was innately balancing his brain's chemistry. Her desire was for Jonathan to have a fighting chance in healing most completely using his brain's natural chemistry for wellness.

"Imagine yourself in the warm, energizing sunshine. Allow yourself to feel relaxed. Your grandma tells me that you understand about battery-powered toys. Your body needs energy so that it can heal. Just like a toy needs a battery to move, your body creates its own energy so it can move. It works kind of like that battery–operated toy bear of mine needed to move. The battery created energy."

Jonathan continued to stay relaxed. He breathed calmly through his nose with his mouth closed. Jonathan was lucky that he could breathe by himself without a ventilator. There were other children in HWH that needed ventilators to breathe. Susan felt fortunate her young client could breathe by himself. Telling him a simple story helped him understand the value of resting. She continued telling him this brief story.

"I'd like you to get some energy. Once you create energy for yourself by resting and sleeping, you'll feel better. After you recharge your batteries, you'll have power so we can keep working and you can get better faster. We know that you can hear us now. You've made great progress. So just for now, if you agree to sleep, and build your energy up, we can visit later. I'm glad you figured out how to talk with us using your wonderful smile."

There was no response from Jonathan after she spoke with him. She went over and turned off the cassette player.

"Augh!" cried Jonathan within about a minute of the cassette player being turned off. We all looked at each other with surprised looks on our faces.

"I wonder if he wants the tape to continue playing?" Susan rhetorically asked the mob. Susan turned the cassette player back on, and Jonathan quickly settled down. "I guess he wants the tape to continue playing." Susan said chuckling for a second.

"I guess he does." concurred Sandra.

"Do you want to sleep?" Susan asked Jonathan. But he just lay there with closed eyes and a Mona Lisa smile painted across his face.

"I think that means yes." Susan surmised.

Susan got up from the chair she had been sitting in and moved away from Jonathan's bed. Everyone followed her. "It's obvious he's interested in doing what it takes to get better. Let's let him sleep and I'll go home for lunch. Maybe we should all take this time to have lunch."

They all stood around for a moment not really knowing what to do. Then Susan said, "I have a client this afternoon. So, I'll come back and work with him tomorrow. For now, I think we have a confirmation that he's in there and he knows we're here."

"Yes, I think were on the right track." accepted everyone.

"See you all tomorrow. For now, working in the morning would probably be best for Jonathan. If you want to come back this afternoon and visit with him, I think he would like that. But I would just let him know that you're here without doing more mental work. He may feel exhausted after the work we've done today. I'll be back at 10 AM tomorrow."

Nancy hugged Susan goodbye. "Thank you so much for sticking in there."

Tim shook Susan's hand saying, "Yes, thank you. I feel encouraged and I appreciate your time."

Susan smiled and started walking down the stairs with Sandra following her close behind. She got to the bottom of the stairs and was close to the door when Sandra stopped her and said, "Susan, I want to apologize for my initial skepticism about hypnosis. I've already learned a lot from you."

"Forget it." Susan said as she put her hand on the backdoor's doorknob. "We've just begun this journey together. We are all on the same team for Jonathan. As long as we focus on doing things to improve his quality of life, we'll be okay."

Susan smiled again and walked out the door. As she walked toward her truck, she said out loud, "Heckuva day, God. I feel like I'm walking on clouds. Thank you for showing me your grace and allowing me to be part of this story." And with that, she got into her vehicle, started it up and drove toward home to get ready for her afternoon client.

Chapter Twelve
Who We Really Are

The next morning, Susan met Nancy and Tim at HWH as agreed. They stayed downstairs and sat in the lower floor conference room. Susan wanted to instruct Nancy and Tim with some important information for Jonathan's wellness.

"Before I move forward with Jonathan's wellness training, I'd like to show you something most people don't know or don't understand about the body."

"All right." agreed Nancy as both Nancy and Tim gave Susan their undivided attention. They all sat down in some comfortable chairs.

"In church, scriptures teach us that we are eternal beings. This is often a difficult concept for people to wrap their mind around. To explain this idea more fully, imagine that it's wintertime. You put gloves on your hand to keep your hands warm."

"What does that have to do with being an eternal being?" Tim jumped in.

"I'm getting to that." Susan offered. "Just listen for a minute while I suggest a visual to make things easier to comprehend."

"Okay."

"Imagine that your hand represents you as an eternal or a spiritual being. And the glove represents the human being part of you."

"I don't understand." confessed Tim with a puzzled look on his face.

"Neither do I, really…" agreed Nancy.

"Okay, can you understand that earth life is a temporary existence? That's why the human body is called mortal."

Tim and Nancy looked at Susan blankly.

"Okay, let's do it this way. Picture giving Jonathan a battery-powered toy. Can the toy move without the battery?"

"That's easy." affirmed Tim. "It's the battery that makes the toy move."

"Okay. Good. You get that, too, Nancy?"

"Yes, I understand that idea. The battery is what makes the toy go."

"Correct. All right now…toy manufacturing engineers designed the toy. And the toy is manufactured out of physical materials. The engineers design the toy to move or be animated. Are you with me?"

"Yes." agreed Tim and Nancy looking like young children hearing an interesting story.

"To animate the toy, it needs a battery. The materials the toy is made of include wiring and circuitry can make the toy move. Still with me?"

Tim and Nancy nodded their heads affirmatively.

"Okay let's recap… We're talking about a toy that is animated by a battery. The battery is an energy or power source. We've already established that the toy can only move when the battery is positioned in such a way that it connects with the wiring and circuitry in the toy. As long as the "on/off" switch is in the "on" position the toy moves around or otherwise operates according to its design."

"I've got that." patiently offered Tim. "Toy…power source…toy goes."

"Right. Now let's compare what I just said to the human experience. Humans don't actually exist. We are spiritual, "energetic wave" beings having a human experience. What looks like a solid life form called the human being, is actually densely packed intelligent energy." Susan continued.

"The human being has a power source we call the Spirit animating or giving power to the human form of life. The spirit is what animates or empowers the human being. Without the Spirit version of you, the human version of you would be unable to move around or be alive. Each human is actually two life forms in one; a human being and a spiritual being. The spiritual being is the one that lives on forever. The human being is mortal and is animated for a temporary time period."

"Okay…" started Nancy.

"If you could actually see down to the tiniest building block of what makes up a human "being" you would see that the human is actually made up of intelligent energy. A molecule, atom or particle of a human being is actually densely packed energy vibrating at a specific frequency. AND, a human is made up of intelligent material much like a toy is made up of material that vibrates and stays together because of energetic laws of attraction. For human beings, without the spirit animating the human life form, the human could not "be" or exist as a mortal human. Instead, we would no longer be human we would simply be the REAL being called Spirit."

"Whoa! This is getting way too deep and scientific for me to understand." objected Tim.

"Goodness. Let me see if I understand this correctly. You're saying that each human is actually two life forms in one." slowly started Nancy.

"That's correct." confirmed Susan.

"We have a living battery that's called the spirit that animates the earth form of us which is called a human being." continued Nancy.

"Very good!" smiled Susan. "You really got that quickly."

"I'm lost." confessed Tim. "What are you two talking about?"

"Keep up, Tim. The Pastor did tell us about this in church."

"I must have been sleeping during that sermon."

Nancy and Susan laughed.

"Would you like to have some evidence of your spirit energy?" asked Susan.

"Sure!" enthusiastically said Nancy.

"Okay, here's a simple exercise I do with my clients so they can understand this concept of the duality of life. Just for a minute, rub your hands together."

All three adults sat comfortably in their chairs at a table in the downstairs conference room rubbing their hands together. Tim and Nancy sat in chairs right next to each other.

"Okay, now very gently pull your hands apart leaving a space of about 2 inches between your palms. What do you feel in that space that seems empty?"

"It's warm…" started Tim.

"It feels tingly and warm to me." offered Nancy.

"That's weird. I never did that before." mumbled Tim barely audible.

"Now pay attention to the feeling between your hands because that's the REAL you, the eternal spirit version of you." continued Susan. "That's the vibrational you."

"The vibrational me? Hmmm…" innocently pondered Tim.

"Fascinating!" expressed Nancy in awe as she learned about her spirit energy.

"All right, now shake your hands out a little bit and intend to disconnect. Silently in your mind simply say 'I, the human version of me, disconnect a little from my own spirit vibration a little bit.' Let me know when you're done disconnecting a little bit from your own spirit vibration."

"I'm done." said Tim.

"Me, too." chimed in Nancy.

"Okay now rub your hands together again. But this time after your done rubbing your hands together, instead of putting your hands close together to your own hands, sit closer to each other and put your hands up against each other's palms. Make sure to leave a space in between each other's palms. What do you feel? Go ahead and move your chairs so you're facing each other."

Nancy and Tim turned and faced each other and started the exercise.

"The space between my hands still feels warm to me," started Tim, "but Nancy's energy feels a little bit different than mine."

"Tim's energy is hot, much hotter than mine but it still feels tingly in that open space." noticed Nancy.

"Interesting isn't it?" confirmed Susan.

"Yes! I never knew I could do this." said Tim with an intrigued voice.

"Goodness! I never did anything like this before in church."

"Okay now go ahead and shake your hands out again. This time, we'll form a circle between the three of us." said Susan as she rolled her chair next to Tim and Nancy. "Let's each one of us rub our hands together. Now, let's each one of us put the palms of our hands up against each other's'."

Tim, Nancy and Susan sat in their chairs in a small circle with their palms up against each other's without touching each other's palm touching their spirit hands to each other's.

"Tim and Nancy, what do you notice?"

"I notice that your energy, Susan, feels much different than Nancy's or mine. It's tingly and soft!" revealed Tim.

"Goodness, Susan, your energy feels velvety soft and tingly and Tim's feels very comfortable and reassuring. I've never experienced anything quite like this. It's divine!"

"Truer words were never spoken, Nancy. And in between your hands you can actually change the vibration of your spirit and how it affects your human form. During hypnosis, if you allow yourself to tap into your spirit energy, you can bless yourself with wellness in varying ways. It's all done by your intention using words, thoughts, feelings and even mind images. All that causes a fluctuation in your spirit energy."

"You can?"

"Yes, and I'd like to teach you even more so that you can understand how I'm working with Jonathan's energy. All I'm doing is communicating with him on a vibrational level. The reason why hypnosis is possible and why all life is possible is done by focusing on nurturing wellness. It's all done according to something called the science of vibrational matching."

"Vibrational matching…goodness." started Nancy.

"You've both heard a tuning fork vibrate and let out a sound? Well, actually all life works the same way by vibrational matching. The more we focus on doing and saying things in a loving, kind, gentle manner the more we support and nurture and nourish wellness. Vibrational matching for our purposes is done by vibration of the words and our touch. And this is what I do with all of my clients when it comes to hypnosis and the work that I do."

"Well, I never learned any of this in school." began Tim.

"It's true that you may not have been taught about vibrational matching in school with regard to hypnosis. But nonetheless all life is based on the science of vibrational matching." explained Susan.

Tim and Nancy looked at each other intrigued and in awe of what they had just experienced.

"And what's even more astounding to me is that the human body is actually a nonliving, animated energy body. But that's good news because what the pastor taught us in church is actually true. We never die, we simply transition from frequency to frequency."

"What exactly does that mean?" asked Nancy tilting her head to the right and eyeing Susan suspiciously.

"That means that in Jonathan's situation what we're working to do is have him reanimate his physical energy body using his spirit being to generate wellness for him. I will be asking the human version of him to communicate with the human versions of us. Depending on how Jonathan understands my hypnotic suggestions, he'll react or respond in a way for him to start communicating with us again. That will make life easier for him. Our focus is to improve the quality of life for him."

"At least that's the hope." offered Tim.

"That's the hope." agreed Susan. "His success in communicating with the outside world again is all dependent upon God and Jonathan working together for Jonathan's highest divine purpose. This only happens because Jonathan has free will. Depending upon what God wants for Jonathan and upon what Jonathan wants for himself, we'll see him change or stay the same."

"Amen." said Nancy and Tim in unison.

"That means this is all going to be a trial and error experience. I've got to figure out when he's consciously aware, what parts of his brain can grasp what I say and what to say in the right way for him to respond in a way favorable to Jonathan."

"This could take some time…" suggested Tim.

"This could take a lot of time. So, by us working together, Jonathan's got more of a fighting chance to get better."

Nancy and Tim sat there for a bit absorbing everything that Susan had said.

"This is a lot to take in. It was very interesting going through that rubbing of the hands exercise." shared Tim.

"Your brain is actually like a radio station. You know how you can hear a broadcast when you tune into a certain radio station frequency?"

"Yes." responded both Nancy and Tim.

"Well, your brain actually sends and receives or emits brain waves. Other living creations receive and send intelligent thought waves back. You've heard of people talking to plants? And they do much better when they hear loving words in a loving tone? That's because a human, when thinking thoughts and speaking them out loud, is sending a wave of intelligent energy. That's why prayer works. And because you are two beings in one, you always have a direct connection to God. So, you use the human version of you and spiritual version of you when you think. We really are very powerful beings. And since science has proven the duality exists, doesn't it make sense to learn how to effectively use hypnosis and thought energy in an uplifting, constructive way?"

"Wow. This seems like we're in an episode of the Twilight Zone." softly said Tim.

They all laughed and Susan said, "I know this seems like we live according to science fiction. Let's go through one more exercise and then we can go up and see Jonathan. This next exercise might be equally intriguing to you."

Nancy and Tim were Susan's captive audience. "Rub your hands together once more. Put your hands up next to each other's like before leaving a space in between your hands." instructed Susan.

The loving couple who had been married for about 50 years obediently complied. As they held their hands across from each other, they smiled and looked lovingly into each other's eyes.

"Now Tim, as your hands are up close to Nancy think and feel love toward Nancy. Intentionally feel love for her. Nancy, describe what you feel in the space between your hands and Tim's hands."

"I feel a gentle warm feeling between Tim and I, the kind of feeling I feel when he's hugging me or kissing me. It feels like deep abiding love... like he cherishes me. It's unmistakably Tim's energy."

Tim smiled and confessed, "Because that's what I feel for you."

"Okay, now you Nancy, feel love for Tim. And as she does Tim, describe what you feel in the space between your hands and Nancy's hands."

"It's like a warm gentle breeze, soft, velvety, genuine... it's Nancy good vibrations. It's is undeniably my Nancy's spirit energy!"

"Okay, now as the both of you are enjoying this genuinely loving feeling between each other, what's one thing that's very meaningful for the both of you? This idea would be something unmistakable shared between the two of you. It would be something that's of great interest to both of you like the gentle feel of rain against your face, or the sound of lovely birds singing. Or perhaps it could be the aroma of something the two of you share that's significant for both of you."

"Cotton candy!" they said in unison chuckling.

"Cotton candy?" Susan asked.

"Yes, it's kind of a joke between both of us. When we were in high school together, we loved sharing cotton candy. Tim would buy one cotton candy. First, he would take a bite, then I would take a bite. When we saw there was one bite left, we would both bite into it and finish the empty paper tube by kissing each other through the last bite. Our lips would meet and we would really relish that last bite. We still do it. It's our little thing we do once a year usually around our anniversary." lovingly shared Nancy with a shy smile.

"That's sweet. Now here's something really wonderful. If you choose, you can have cotton candy as your own special symbol. Think of the cotton candy memory as you have rehearsed it here in this exercise. Recall the aroma, and the intensity of that final kiss at the end of the role. This can be your special symbol that conveys your love for each other. Practice making this your special symbol memory. You can use it as a communication device between the two of you."

"What do you mean a communication device?" asked Tim.

"Most likely, after you've completed your earth missions, one of you will survive the other. Not intending to freak you out or anything but suppose Tim returns back to the spirit realm first. He'll be waiting for you Nancy in the etheric home once again. It's a natural progression."

"Go on." said Nancy.

"When you want to communicate with Tim you can use the cotton candy memory as a communication device between the two of you. By setting up the symbol now, you can see there is nothing to fear when the time comes to make your transition back into our real home, the spiritual world." revealed Susan.

"Little lost here, Susan." said Tim.

"Okay, this is taking a little bit longer and your hands might be feeling a little tired right now. So, put your hands down in your laps for a moment and rest your arms. Here's how it would be." continued Susan. "Nancy, suppose Tim is gone back to the spirit world. And you Nancy are still living the human experience. Let's say you'd like to share a moment with Tim. What you would do is connect to a loving memory of you sharing the cotton candy with Tim in your mind. You would feel relaxed and calm doing this. You sit with her hands palms up remembering the cotton candy memory."

"Okay…" happily obeyed Nancy.

"Now Tim, suppose you are no longer animating the human version of you. You are the spirit you, the real you in the spiritual realm now. You can communicate with Nancy through your hands."

"How would I do that?"

"Understand that this is a rehearsal right now, but Tim, wave your human hands without touching the human skin of

Nancy's human hands. You're moving the energy in that space above Nancy's human hands. Wave your hands up and down above Nancy's hands. Nancy, can you feel the fluctuations in the energy space above your hands?"

"Yes. I can feel that."

"Okay, for now, because right now both versions, the human version and the spiritual version of Tim is here, both versions are moving in that space. But it is Tim's spiritual version that is moving and causing the fluctuation in the space above your human hand's skin. Once Tim crosses over, after you've connected with Tim, let it be known and agreed to by both of you that when you feel a fluctuation in the space that's Tim communicating using his spirit energy. And when the both of you consciously recall the cotton candy memory, you'll both be connecting with that special symbol."

"Goodness!" exclaimed Nancy. "Rose is going to love this."

"And what you can do Nancy, is ask Tim simple yes and no questions. Let it be known that the energy fluctuation of Tim's unique energy frequency which you are now acquainted with will mean a 'yes' response to your question. And when there is no movement in that space between your hands, that will mean a 'no' response."

"This is going to be very helpful when the time comes." said Nancy. "I know the chances are that I will outlive Tim."

"Hey, wait a minute. I just might outlive you!"

"In any event, this is a simple way that you can communicate once whomever crosses over first passes on." continued Susan.

"I won't feel so lonely knowing that I can communicate with Tim using this simple exercise." smiled Nancy.

"I'm so glad that we met you, Susan." said Tim. "You are a wealth of information we've never heard anywhere else."

"Okay, I'm sure this is a lot for you to absorb. I encourage you to practice being intimately familiar with each other's spiritual energy frequency signature."

"I think that's a great idea." agreed Tim.

"I hope you can really help Jonathan recover from this horrible accident." confided Nancy.

"Nancy, I'll do my best to write more hypnosis scripts that work for him. I feel very hopeful that he wants to improve the quality of his life. You do understand I'm here to assist him on his earth the journey rather than try to convince or persuade him to do something against his conscious wishes."

"What do you mean?"

"Well, as I think I've already explained, everything is up to Jonathan. We'll see what he wants to do with his life. My focus is on improving the quality of his life by suggesting ideas he can have peace of mind. Peace of mind is priceless in my opinion. But it's up to God to heal him. It is by his faith in God and in doing his own thinking that he can improve the quality of his life."

"Oh, I understand that."

"Some people think that a hypnotist has control over them. But nothing can be further from the truth. Just as I have no ability to digest his food for him, Jonathan is in complete control of his thinking. I can suggest what I think are constructive ideas that might not have ever occurred to him. However, it is Jonathan who thinks his version of the individual thoughts I suggest."

"Yes, and I would never have it any other way." confirmed Nancy.

"Each of us sees life from his or her individual viewpoint. It is by being a unique individual that adds variety and enriches the world."

"That's why Nancy and I are so compatible." offered Tim.

"Exactly." affirmed Susan.

"I know full well believe that every time I would climb a tree and get ready to cut it down, she was never crazy about me being a tree feller. But she went along with it anyway. She knew it was just something that I had to do as a part of my life."

"So, you figured that out, huh? You knew that I felt afraid you might get seriously hurt every time you went to work?" asked Nancy turning toward Tim and subtly slipping her soft hand into his calloused one.

"I knew…but I also knew that you knew I was careful. And that a part of me would've died if I had to have a nine to five office job."

"You're right. I knew that." Nancy leaned over toward Tim and gave him an endearing peck on the cheek.

"All right, all right. Now let's not get all emotionally sloppy. We're keeping Susan from working with Jonathan." voiced Tim feigning an objection to Nancy's public display of affection.

"Okay then. I think it's time for me to spend some time with Jonathan."

The three of them stood up from their chairs and walked upstairs to Jonathan's room. Embraced in a cloud of spiritual bliss from their experience with Susan, Tim and Nancy felt like they were walking on air.

"Blurgg!" erupted vomit like an active volcano from the young boy.

"He's been having an extended bout of nausea and vomiting this morning." offered Nurse Pierson.

Nancy, Tim and Susan all looked at each other with disbelief.

"Maybe the next script I'll write for him will be one specifically to recommend calm digestion." suggested Susan. "It can be popped into the recorder for times just like this."

Nancy and Tim slowly followed Susan as she walked over to Jonathan's bedside where Sandra Pierson continued to tend to him while he worked through another bout of vomiting. "Hey, Jonathan… it's your friend Susan."

Sandra stepped back and stood by Tim and Nancy who were near Jonathan's bed. They watched as Susan spoke lovingly to Jonathan.

Susan sat down in one of the chairs by Jonathan's bedside. She leaned down close to her client and started to speak in soft tones in his ear. "Listen to my voice and let your body relax. Your grandma and grandpa are here with me now, too. They love you very much." Susan began.

She continued using a quiet, soothing voice as she coached Jonathan to relax his body so he could naturally feel comfortable again. "The nurse her name is Sandra, put some liquid food into a tube that goes directly into your stomach. In order for you to have power to get better, use the liquid food you took into your body through the feeding tube. Use it to get power and energy to feel better." she said.

Susan stopped talking for a moment and looked at Jonathan to see if something changed. It didn't, but she kept talking to him in a low, soft, gentle voice. "There is a word people use for letting food give them power. It is called nourishing. When you think or say the word nourish, that means you are giving your body power and getting better. Let the liquid food in and use the food to nourish your body, Jonathan. Relax your body. Allow your body to be calm. You are in charge here." The coma whispering hypnotist saw no outward changes in Jonathan's behavior except that he was calming down.

"When you choose to calm your body, you can easily nourish yourself using the food. Relax and use the food to nourish your body."

Susan continued to speak softly in Jonathan's ear. As Jonathan listened to Susan speaking in soft, quiet tones, he accepted her suggestions.

"Look at how he's relaxing." whispered Sandra to Nancy. Then, she gasped. "Look! He opened his eyes."

"Yes, I see that."

"And he's stopped vomiting." added Tim.

After a while, she said, "Jonathan, your grandma and grandpa are going to visit with you for a while now."

Jonathan looked directly at Susan. And he smiled.

"I'm going to go to my office and start working on a new story for you to hear. I'll record it on tape. In a new program, use the ideas and quiet your stomach when you hear the story ideas. I'll return again soon. Then you'll have this tape for calming your stomach. Remember everything I just said. You'll feel better soon."

Jonathan started to cry.

"I think Jonathan wants Susan to stay." said Tim to Nancy. "I think he's crying as a way to communicate with her and tell her he wants her to stay."

Gently stroking one of his cheeks before she got up to leave, Susan suggested, "Every time your cheek is stroked instantly you feel calm and relaxed and you can feel good about what's happening for yourself. Remember, Jonathan, any time your cheek is stroked, you feel calm and relaxed and can solve any thinking project."

Whispering back to Tim, Nancy said, "I think you're right."

"Jonathan, I see that you're crying. I think you might be feeling afraid I won't come back. I promise I will come back. If you understand that I will come back calm yourself and stop crying. This will be a signal to me that you understood what I said."

In a short amount of time, Jonathan stopped crying. Susan stroked his cheek again. "So, I see that you understood what I said, Jonathan. Thank you for talking to me and letting me know you understood that I will come back."

Jonathan looked at Susan again and smiled weakly.

"It's going to be okay, Jonathan. I'm going to my office and go to work for you. In the meantime, think in a way that's helpful to you. I will record some new stories for you. They are actually called thinking projects. You understand them by thinking about the story ideas." said Susan.

Susan's client closed his eyes for a moment, then opened them again looking directly at her.

"Maybe you forgot what I just said so I'll say it again. It's okay if you need me to remind you right now about what I just said. You are very smart and you are getting better and better every day. I'm going home to create some new thinking projects for you so you can help yourself even more than you already have. I will be back soon."

Jonathan closed his eyes and looked like he was starting to feel tired. Susan continued to speak to him in that soft, low tone. "Remember that Sandra and grandma and grandpa are here. You are safe and in a bed. Remember you are safe and in a bed where people care about you." Before she left, Susan stroked Jonathan's cheek again and calmly said, "Jonathan I will be back soon. Any time your cheek is stroked instantly you feel calm and can think happy thoughts."

The hypnotist stood up and addressed Tim, Nancy and Sandra who were standing by Jonathan's bedside. "Would you all meet me out in the hall for just a moment?"

Jonathan started to cry and his body tensed when Susan stood up. He opened his eyes wide and looked right at Susan. Nancy looked at Susan with a helpless look for an instance and then slid into the chair by Jonathan's bedside.

"Jonathan, it's Grandma." said Nancy. Then, she gently stroked Jonathan's cheek with her hand. She started speaking in quiet tones to Jonathan. "Every time your cheek is stroked instantly you feel calm and can think happy thoughts. We're going out into the hall for a moment. It's all okay. We'll be back."

After a short time, Jonathan calmed down.

"I feel confident he heard you, Nancy." said Susan.

Once assembled out in the hall, Susan talked with all of Jonathan's other caregivers. "Here's what I just did. As you all saw, Jonathan DID hear me. I asked him to stop crying and calm himself and he did. And then Nancy, you did the same thing. It's good that you did the cheek stroking. And I'd like everyone to use the cheek stroking from now on to connect with Jonathan. I believe consistency is very important for him."

"Yes, I believe he did consciously respond to you… which is impressive." said Sandra.

"You are quite a coma whisperer. I never thought a person in coma or vegetative
    state could give a conscious response. But you've just shown me that they can respond. You just have to know what their actions mean."

"If I haven't already clearly told you, I believe Jonathan's vegetative state is evidence of him being in a deep hypnotic state. And it's probably necessary to repeat things a lot because of memory impairment. But of course, I'm doing a lot of guessing here. I think it's very important to be extremely patient and have low memory and comprehension expectations at first. That's why I think it's necessary to repeat things a lot. I think in his own way he'll let us know when he understands our messages."

"I still don't really understand how hypnosis works." said Nancy.

"As you saw, I suggested to Jonathan that anytime his cheek is stroked he can easily feel in control again during any life situation. I formatted the hypnotic suggestion in such a way that if he or anybody else stroked his cheek, he could use that physical action of the cheek stroking as a reminder to think the situation through. I am looking for simple ways he can improve a current yet temporarily unpleasant feeling situation. I think from his viewpoint, things may look very distorted. So, I think it's vital we need to be very patient with him. Hypnosis is a normal and natural nervous system phenomenon. When you work WITH it, you can effortlessly achieve goals."

"Well, I still have a lot to understand about it but whatever it is, it's working. That's all I care about. In any event," agreed Nancy, "patience is going to be very helpful for him."

"When we stay focused on what we CAN do according to what makes sense to him, we provide sensory stimulation so he can create new neural pathways for wellness."

"And so sensory stimulation is important for him." said Tim.

"Yes, very important. When I was working with his self-created hypnotic trance, I specifically formatted a hypnotic suggestion and suggested that each program now has a label. That helps him more easily identify what's happening by giving it a name. That's why I called the first tape a thinking project. And when Nancy also used cheek stroking, that was good for him."

"A thinking project…" said Nancy. "I like that."

"People like working on projects. We see projects as a challenge and challenges can be fun. I specifically avoided using the word 'problem' because problems seem tedious and too much like work. So, I'm going to ask you to avoid using the word 'problem' when talking with him. Just refer to each hypnotic program tape as a thinking project program to help him achieve specific goals."

"What about the current hypnosis tape?"

"Well, now that we know he can hear us I think you can use all tapes with headphones for him to calm himself. Using the tape with headphones, the nurses can come into the room without getting hypnotized themselves."

"That would be very helpful for my staff." agreed Sandra.

"What I'm doing is using Jonathan's level of understanding to build new neural pathways and hopefully help him improve and build upon his communication skills. What I'd like him to do is work from the inside out."

"Should I be taking notes about what you're saying?" asked Nancy.

"If you want to. Like I was saying early on, it may be helpful for you to keep a journal. I'm asking Jonathan to visualize and mentally rehearse from the inside out how to feel powerful by using his own thoughts. As he uses his inner mind images as a model to achieve goals that improve his situation, this gives him a sense of control."

"And when he feels in control, he's gonna naturally want to stick with you? Is that it?" asked Tim.

"That's the goal. The mind is very powerful. I'm showing Jonathan how to tap into his own power using his imagination. Eventually, I'm hoping to see him physically stroke his own cheek during times of duress so he can calm himself."

"Goodness! That would truly be a miracle." confirmed Nancy.

"In sessions with other clients, I suggest to them ways that they can feel a sense of control over their external situations by imagining being in a place where they feel in control or happy. This place is from within their own mind instead of by looking to be told what to think or feel by watching another human being. You all saw that he calmed himself after I spoke very softly in his ear and stroked his cheek, correct?"

"Yes." said Sandra.

"Well, that's something that's meaningful to him then. Using the cheek stroking works for him. I'm hoping to eventually see him do it himself. So, I'm asking you Nancy and Tim to pray that cheek stroking will be something he eventually does to help himself."

"I'll pray for him, too." said Sandra.

"Thank you." said both Nancy and Tim.

"Sandra, I want it put in his chart that everyone, even the doctors are to use cheek stroking before they start talking with him. Even if he's calm, I think it's important. I'm going to talk with his doctors and require them to do it, too, before any doctor exams."

"I will put it in the chart, Mrs. Wallace."

"I'll create two more tapes… One to reduce nausea and vomiting and another one for general stress relief. Whenever he needs to calm himself, gently stroke one of his cheeks and he'll start to think for himself… at least that's the intention… in calming ways. I'll include the cheek stroking suggestion in his taped programs." said Susan.

"How will we know if the cheek stroking will always work?" asked Sandra.

"At first, I expect to see subtle changes in his behavior. I'm looking for things to improve at his level and his speed. As I said before, his progress is all up to Jonathan and God. This might be as good as it gets. However, I feel very hopeful because he's already responding so well after hearing the first tape."

"How long will it take you to write these next two tapes?"

"I'll get started writing them after I get back to my office. I should have them done in a day or two. I think he's about had it for today." With that, Susan said goodbye for the day.

"Thank you so much for all you taught us today." said Nancy with a smile. And she hugged Susan goodbye for the day. Then, she sat down at Jonathan's bedside.

"Yes, thanks for taking so much time with us today." Tim extended his hand in friendship toward Susan. Susan smiled at Tim, shook his hand goodbye and then, Tim sat down on the other side of Jonathan's bed.

With that, Susan walked out of Jonathan's room toward the facility's parking lot. Time marched on as always. Rose and Nancy marveled at what they were learning along the way.

"That was pretty amazing information Susan shared with you last month." conveyed Rose. "Pass me another cookie, will you?" she said sitting at Nancy's kitchen table sipping herbal tea with her friend.

"Susan has no idea how much peace that information brought to me." said Nancy. "Goodness knows I've always wondered how I might be able to stay connected with Tim when my time comes to go back to our spirit home. Now I believe that if I pass on before Tim does, he and I will still have a way to be able to communicate."

"And vice versa?"

"And vice versa."

"I'm so glad you shared it with me. Practicing with you made it easy for me to understand how to do it myself." said Rose.

"I wish I would've known that spirit energy information before Michael had passed. It's kind of scary and exciting to think I can communicate with Mike again now."

"You two really lived it up when you were married. How long were you two together?"

"Thirty-seven years. And boy did we have a lot of fun. I can't imagine a better mate for me than Mike."

"The two of you went to Europe how many times?"

"Three. We rode bicycles and motorbikes across Europe. But that was when it was much safer than it is nowadays to travel overseas."

"And Mike and those precious show pigeons of his." scoffed Nancy.

"Wait a minute. Mike might have had his quirks because he loved raising pigeons and showing them professionally but what about Tim and his fishing lures? Now does he really need all those fishing lures?"

"I don't know. I don't get it. But I'm sure they have the same kind of things to say about us and our quirks."

There was a pregnant pause until Nancy broke the silence.

"Well, have you connected with Mike yet now that he's on the other side?"

"I have."

"You have?"

"Yes."

"How do you know it was Mike?"

"Because I asked 'yes' and 'no' questions and actually felt his spirit hands waving above my human hands in response. I could feel the energy waves. I'm sure of it."

"WOW!"

"Yeah."

"What did you ask him?"

"Well, you know what, I'm just going to leave that between me and Mike. But I will tell you, his answers did make me feel kind of perky..."

"I know. You're saying it's none of my business because it's probably X-rated knowing you and Mike."

"Uh, so I see you finally finished that Seahawks afghan. Very nice."

Nancy wrinkled up her nose at Rose. Rose wrinkled her nose back at Nancy which was Rose's signal for 'none of your business but yes you're right.'

The two longtime friends finished their tea and cookies. "Are you ready to go see Jonathan?" asked Nancy. "He's made some progress over the past four weeks. Using those two tapes have really made a difference for him. Susan thinks it's time to try something new today."

"What is she going to do?"

"I don't know. But look at the clock. We're supposed to meet her there in about fifteen minutes. We better hurry." And with that, the two ladies put their teacups and saucers in the kitchen sink at Nancy's house. They were eager to get to HWH.

"Hello, Mrs. Wallace." said Sandra smiling broadly. "Mrs. Hamilton. It's a great day, isn't it?"

"Sure. What's the latest with my grandson? And we're probably going to be here for a while so just call me Nancy."

"And just continue to call me Mrs. Hamilton. It makes me feel powerful."

Nancy looked at her friend, Rose with big eyes and a grin.

"Oh, all right. Just call me Rose." said Rose smiling.

"Well, Nancy and Rose, Jonathan's eyes are open more and more. I think he really likes all the colors of the television when we put it in his room and leave it on for a while."

"Goodness." said Nancy. "His eyes are open more and more! Wow!"

"Susan is up there now working with him. Before she came in today, I told him that she was coming to visit with him. He brightened right up and smiled knowing she was coming. I would have never guessed that hypnosis could be so helpful for someone in vegetative state."

Nancy put her hand on Sandra's arm. "This is exciting! He's getting better."

Rose and Nancy scurried up the stairs to see Jonathan. They walked into Jonathan's room to see Susan sitting by his bedside.

Jonathan's fingers and toes were contracted and rigid. It was something that happens sometimes for people who have massive brain damage.

"Now Jonathan, I'm going to touch your elbow. I can feel that the muscles in your arms are very tense. Just relax your arm."

Jonathan spontaneously opened his eyes and then closed them. His breathing continued to sound very watery. Fluid in his lungs seemed consistently problematic for him.

He turned his gaze away from Susan for a moment. Then he awkwardly opened his eyes again and closed them. It was almost as if his eyelids were impaired by something sticky.

Susan put her hand on Jonathan's elbow and felt it relax. "That's very good, Jonathan. I just felt you relax your arm."

Nancy and Rose smiled at each other. Susan smiled from ear to ear and raised her eyebrows in delight knowing Jonathan was still consciously responding.

Angela, another one of Jonathan's nurses, suddenly walked into the room. She casually strolled over to Jonathan's bed and announced, "Hi, Jonathan. It's me, Angela. Hi, Jonathan. It's me, Angela. Hi, Jonathan. It's me, Angela. I'm here to check your diaper."

Unexpectedly, Jonathan tensed his body up. He started to cry.

"Do you want Angela to leave? Would you rather stay in your dirty diaper?" asked Susan.

Suddenly, Jonathan quieted right down.

"Jonathan? If you understood what I just said, smile for me."

In a few seconds, Jonathan smiled.

"Jonathan? If you stay in your soiled diaper, you could get a rash. Jonathan, if you stay in your soiled diaper, you could get a rash. That could hurt. That could hurt. Is that what you want?"

Jonathan started to tense his body.

"Jonathan, I noticed that you just tensed your body up. If you will let Angela change your diaper, then we can get back to working with each other. So, if you calm your body, I'll know you understood me. If you calm your body, I'll know you understood me. I will know that it is all right for Angela to change your diaper."

After Susan talked with Jonathan about getting the diaper changed, stroking his cheek and barely talking in calming, quiet, gentle tones, Jonathan calmed down. Susan was coma whispering really, a word Susan created that really meant she was communicating to her young friend in vegetative state. Jonathan was really in vegetative state rather than in a coma state. He was coming back to consciousness by her conveying ideas sometimes barely audible to even those around him. It was the way she communicated with him. Her gentle voice inflection, her voice tone and her genuine caring. That was what he consciously responded to.

He knew she was there for him on an intimately spiritual level. It was something that transcended human communication. It was genuine love, eternal love. The kind of love only God gives to us. Somehow, she allowed God's love to flow through her to him. She wanted Jonathan to know that there was an eternal bond that would always be there even after he had completed his earth journey. It was like a mother's love for her son, the same type of love she shared with her own son, Jason.

"I'm very grateful that the doctors are supportive of the cheek stroking and hypnosis. Goodness, we're certainly learning a lot about seeing miracles from Jonathan." said Nancy.

"Now if we can just get the excess fluid in his lungs under control that would be great." said Angela. She stood nearby Jonathan's bed as she verbally made her comment.

"Would you step out into the hall with me for just a minute?" said Nancy to Angela. The two women stepped out into the hall for a minute outside of Jonathan's hearing range. "Angela, when you speak about Jonathan, only talk about what he can do, please. Don't talk about fluid on his lungs or anything else negative. It's discouraging."

"Oh! You're absolutely right, Mrs. Wallace. I wasn't thinking about what I was saying. I'll pay closer attention from now on."

"Thank you, Angela."

The two women stepped back into Jonathan's room. The air in the room was light and happy even though Jonathan felt unhappy about being in his diaper.

"Jonathan, you're my little miracle boy." said Rose. She clasped her hands together feeling very happy to see his progress as did the rest of the women.

"I think Jonathan is ready for you to start reading him stories from books." said Susan. "Keep the stories simple and choose ones you already know are his favorites. This will be good brain stimulation for him."

"What about playing the two new taped programs you made for him? Should we continue to play those when the need arises?" asked Nancy.

"In my opinion, we should continue to do what seems to work for him until it stops working. Jonathan is a brilliant young boy. He will let us know what he likes I'm sure."

"Yes, I'm sure he will." said Nancy.

"Well, I think you should spend some time with him, Rose for now. How about it? Want to read a story to him?"

"I would love to read a story to him." smiled Rose. She grabbed a copy of one of his favorite stories and sat down next to him. She leaned over and stroked his cheek and said, "Jonathan, it's me, Rose. Going to read you a story right now. Jonathan, it's me, Rose. I'm going to read your story right now."

Jonathan looked directly at Rose and smiled. She opened up the book then started to read. Angela stayed for a while but then was called away to tend to another child. Nancy sat down in the chair on the other side of Jonathan and listened as Rose read to her grandson. She felt very hopeful that Jonathan would continue to improve. Jonathan, Rose, Nancy, Tim and Phil continued living their lives as best they could.

"You see, Phil, I'm spending a lot of time with Jonathan now. This hypnotist, Susan, she has made it possible for us to communicate with Jonathan on more than a human level. He's actually getting better."

"What?"

"Jonathan… getting better… using hypnosis." said Tim.

"That's good."

"I'm hoping that by this time next year, I might even be able to take Jonathan out fishing. You never know, it could happen. I really believe it might."

"What might happen?"

"Fishing… with Jonathan… next year."

"Oh. Fishing. That's good."

Tim shook his head. He continued visiting with Phil making the most of the opportunity. "These visits are precious, Phil. Very precious to me. They mean a lot. Not to get emotionally sloppy or anything, but you're a good man, Phil. And you're a good brother. Do you know that I love you?"

Phil smiled.

He knew.

Chapter Thirteen
Getting Through the Daily Tedium

Things were going very well for several weeks at HWH for
Jonathan. The two taped hypnosis programs for general stress
relief and nausea and vomiting worked very well for Jonathan. It
was time for another visit. Susan walked up the stairs to Jonathan's
room and entered overhearing Tim telling Jonathan a story.

"And then that rascally old Never Quits started fighting the
fishing line. Remember? After all those years trying to catch
him...I finally caught him ... and he tugged and he pulled on the
line. I bet he was thinking, 'Oh, hello, Susan."

"Never Quits the fish was thinking about me?!? Wow! My
reputation is well known even in the animal kingdom? I'm really
doing a great marketing job aren't I?"

Tim smiled. "No! I was just reminding Jonathan about the
time we were fishing."

"Don't stop on my account." said Susan to Tim. And Tim
continued telling Jonathan the story.

Just at that moment, Nancy walked into Jonathan's room.
She had been downstairs going over some insurance paperwork for
Jonathan with Sandra. She stood listening to Tim as he continued
telling their grandson the fish story.

"And you, my courageous boy, are as powerful and smart
and brave and smart as Never Quits because you never give up.
Remember how Never Quits was so smart at breaking the fishing
line and he got away? You are like that. You keep on figuring out
how to keep on swimming. You're strong like Never Quits.
You're strong like Never Quits." And then Tim reached down and
stroked Jonathan's cheek and repeated the cheek stroking hypnotic
affirmation. "Every time your cheek is stroked, instantly you
know what thoughts to think to think happy powerful thoughts to
achieve every goal that makes you powerful."

"Tell me Jonathan, if you like this story. Smile and I'll
know that you liked this story." said Grandpa. Jonathan easily
smiled and he looked intently at his Grandpa. You could see the
life in his eyes.

Susan walked over to the other side of the bed and leaned down to say hello to Jonathan. She stroked his cheek and said, "Hello Jonathan, this is Susan. Hello Jonathan, this is Susan. Hello Jonathan, this is Susan. How about we start working on some language skills? Can you say the letter, "A?""

Nancy moved closer to Jonathan's bed waiting to hear Jonathan answer Susan's question. "Mmm…" he grunted unintelligibly.

"That was very good, Jonathan…" said Susan. "Go ahead and make that "A" sound again."

"Mmmm…" he grunted again unintelligibly. Then he started to cry out of frustration.

"You're doing a great job, just like Never Quits! Just keep being smart and using your brain power, Jonathan. Keep being smart and use your brainpower, Jonathan. You can do it." said Susan. She knew Jonathan's intention to speak was there but the brain damage might have been too great. Susan knew it was important to say encouraging things to him even if he was unable to achieve what she wanted him to achieve.

Nancy walked over closer to her grandson and said quietly, "You're doing a great job, Jonathan. Keep up the great work." But Tim could see the disappointment in her face.

"How about I turn on the TV for a little bit, Jonathan? I think Duck Tales are on." Tim turned the TV on and turned Jonathan's body a bit in his bed so he could face the television screen. Nancy walked out into the hall wanting to hide her disappointment from her grandson. Susan got up from Jonathan's bedside and strolled out into the hall. Nancy was standing at the rail looking up at the cathedral ceiling.

Susan stood next to Nancy and looked up at the beautiful ceiling as well and started to speak. "Howya doin'?"

"Goodness, Susan, I see him struggling in there, wanting to do what you ask him to do and it's so hard for him. It gets me in the heart. It's so frustrating. I find myself crying more than I really want to cry."

"You know, as a caregiver, you sometimes feel like you're on your own. I do understand your frustration. However, I encourage you to see how far he's come. You and Tim have come far, too. It is okay for you to ask for help in getting through your frustrations."

"Thanks. Tim was great in there. He is really catching on to doing what's helpful for Jonathan. I've got to be strong for them both. I don't want them to see me crying." said Nancy with tears in her eyes.

"They don't have to see you crying but there's nothing wrong with you letting your feelings out. Understand you are NOT alone. If you tell yourself you are alone and that you ALWAYS have to be strong for everyone, except yourself, you might feel like asking for help is cheating. Do you ever feel like that?"

"Sometimes…"

"Or, do you expect that things should always go your way and that if you don't get what you want for Jonathan that there's something wrong?"

"Seems wrong, doesn't it?"

"We all can tell ourselves those little lies. It's just perfectionistic thinking. Nancy, is there something you could think that reminds you of the truth?"

"The truth?"

"That you are always a priceless child of God?"

"I know I'm always a priceless child of God."

"If you expect to be able to fix everything, when you can't fix something the way you think it needs to be fixed to be 'right', it's impossible to feel like a winner. Scorekeeping against yourself expecting to be all things to all people at all times and to know the right answer every time doesn't work very well does it?"

Nancy shot a look at Susan that said she wanted to talk about something else.

"If you believe the lies you think against yourself, you can't win. When you feel like you can't win, then you really feel all alone."

Looking up at the ceiling and occasionally outside at the beautiful pine trees that were waving in the breeze at the moment, Susan could see tears in Nancy's eyes."

"Are you minimizing all your efforts here? If so, you may feel unappreciated and abandoned. If you tell yourself to believe stories like that and compound those types of stories, things can just go downhill from there. Don't abandon yourself when things don't go your way, Nancy. It's too lonely down there. You are really very well-tended. There ARE angels all around you. And there are people here to help you. You do deserve to ask for help. That's what God is for. He's here to help us...always."

Nancy looked at me pursing her lips together. For some reason, she didn't want to approve of herself and what she'd done to keep Jonathan going. "You are very intuitive. It's as if you know what I'm feeling before I even say what I'm feeling."

"Well, Nancy, I've been around the volleyball court a time or two. I've worked with a lot of people. A lot of my clients have told me their deepest feelings about their struggles. Here's the way I see things when it comes to asking for help. Businesses consult all the time. And if big businesses feel completely comfortable about asking for help, wouldn't it be all right for you to ask for help as well when you really need it?"

Nancy smiled silently and continued listening to Susan.

"I think what you want is for Jonathan to hurry up and heal so he can go on with his life. But that might be an unrealistic expectation. For now, this IS his life. Those unrealistic expectations can be mental traps. And, they can set us up to feel mentally stuck. You are NOT a failure if Jonathan can't physically heal as fast as you'd like him to heal. Healing requires a person to use up a LOT of energy."

"I imagine it does..."

"And we all trap ourselves mentally from time to time. When I get myself into the mental trap of believing that I'm all alone and that nobody understands how I feel about a situation, I go back for myself."

"You trap yourself mentally?"

"Of course, I do. That's part of the human experience. Even though I've had all the training I've had to help others stay positive, I have my days when I say discouraging things to myself."

"Be there for myself…" echoed Nancy.

"Feel comfortable about asking for help when you really need it. That's sometimes hard for me to do, too. Maybe that's why I can identify it in others. If I let my ego lead me down a discouraging trail, I've forgotten there are people here that love and support me. And it seems like I need to 'go to the dark side' on occasion. So, after I'm down low for a few minutes, and I realize it, then I ask myself, 'Okay…now that you've been here, do you want to stay here or do you want to get back up into the light?' And then I do my best to get up. But if I can't get up, I call somebody and talk it out."

"At times it takes all the strength you have to ask for help when you really need it?"

"Exactly."

"Because you don't want to appear weak. You can't be all things to all people at all times. Nobody can."

Nancy was mulling over the things Susan was saying. They both continued looking at the beautiful cathedral ceiling and sighed.

"Nancy, you can only give so much. Allow yourself time to re-energize when you need it. That's how you can continue caregiving for Jonathan. I'm really glad to see Tim taking such an active part in providing sensory stimulation for Jonathan. Even though I don't come here every day, I bet you do. I encourage you to take some time off for yourself occasionally. When you do let Tim contribute and participate in helping Jonathan, it takes the burden off your shoulders. I think it's good for your family, and I'm sure it's good for you when you do this."

"You're probably right."

"Instead of looking at yourself like you're doing something weak when you ask for help, just tell yourself sometimes you have to do things you don't really want to do for the short-term to get what you want for the long term."

"What does that mean?"

"Well, you may be like a lot of women. You do your best to be a superwoman. But there's only one Linda Carter and she was an actress only playing the role of Wonder Woman."

"It's hard watching him in there struggling and yet I know that's his best. I just want him to have some normalcy back in his life. And I also want some normalcy in my life, too. Goodness, that sounds so selfish of me!"

"Being a caregiver is about being in a relationship. Caregiving is all about relationships. You're not being selfish wanting things to be 'normal' again whatever that means to you. You're just acting human. For now, can you see this life routine as your new normal?"

"My new normal?"

"Yes, things may not get much better than they already are, Nancy. So, I encourage you to find a pace that works for you. Take time to re-energize yourself. Think about the person that you're taking care of as changing all the time. But sometimes the change is miniscule. Maybe you can't see it but Jonathan might already be as good as he's going to get."

"I know that everything you're saying is true. There's a part of me that feels so exhausted that I don't even know what I'm thinking."

"There's one more thing I'd like to try and then that might be all I can do. I may no longer need to come here anymore."

"You mean…you're going to abandon us?!"

"I'm not abandoning you but I think I'm very close to doing all that I am able to do. I can come by from time to time but I think I am very close to being done with helping Jonathan as much as I can help him."

Nancy frowned. "You have helped so much. It won't be the same without you."

"Don't write me off yet. Like I said, there is one more thing I'd like to do."

"You're right. I do want to fix everything. Goodness, I still feel so guilty about the whole drowning accident happening."

"Sometimes it's easy to feel guilty and keep yourself stuck in guilt for being unable to fix something that doesn't really need to be fixed. I really think that nothing needs to be fixed here, Nancy. For whatever the reasons, everything is as it should be. God has a plan for us all. You are in that plan He has for you. We may not always understand the plan, but we are all in it. Enjoy life the best you can right now. I encourage you to create happy memories with Jonathan because that's all we can take with us when we leave this earth life."

"Happy memories. That's a good idea. Keep focusing on creating the happiest memories I can."

"Pick the reason for wanting to go on living be that you know things will get easier. Think about how far you all have come from where things were at the start of the accident. When you compare where you've been to where you are now, you can see you've come so far, can't you? In fact, I'm so impressed with your resilience. And that's because of you and Tim and Rose and Angela and Sandra and all the other people that are working with the situation as it is. You all are working with the situation the best you can."

"Being a caregiver isn't for sissies."

"I agree. It's hard work. Give yourself credit for doing an excellent job in a very challenging set of circumstances."

"Thanks. I needed to hear that. It'll make a good entry in my journal."

"Oh, so you are keeping a journal. Is it helping?"

"Yes, it is helping."

"And do you have some wisdom you'd like to share that you're learning as a result of writing in your journal?"

"It's important to focus on what you're doing right now...to be fully present in the moment. If I yearn for yesterday or fear about what might be, I just feel unhappy. I'm doing my best to celebrate the now."

"Interesting..." said Susan pensively. "It sounds like you're learning to play a new role, as a new version of you... a stronger version of you."

"Yes. I guess you're right. I don't really feel very strong. I just feel exhausted."

"Because of the experiences that you now have, can you see that you're a more caring caregiver? Perhaps the way you were before, before this caregiving experience and without these compassionate skills you've developed, you would have never been prepared to be the caregiver you are now…"

"You think I am a good caregiver?"

"What matters is if YOU think you are a good caregiver."

"Well, I do my best to celebrate the times I'm really living in the now moment… so I'm sure I'm a good caregiver. Yes, I'm a good caregiver. I love Jonathan so I'm a good caregiver. He's happy, he's well cared for…yes, I'm a good caregiver."

"Can you see that the learning curve through this life event has made you the strong person that you are today? Do you see that as a result of being the caregiver you are now, you've accessed skills that other people may not have been able to access if they had been Jonathan's primary caregiver? That's admirable."

"Thanks. I think I'm ready to get back in and see Jonathan again."

"BE the joy God wants us to be. Isn't that what the pastor tells us all the time at church? You are the joy in Jonathan's life. Because of you and Tim, Jonathan is still here. I really believe that."

"You are a good person, Susan. You knew exactly what I needed to hear."

"I just read a lot. I think I've done enough work with Jonathan today. Just keep doing what you've been doing. I'm going home now. I'll check in again on Jonathan later. Just remember…stay focused on celebrating each little victory. Never give up hope that through the toughest situations you can see light at the end of the tunnel."

"Okay, I will. I'll see you later."

Susan smiled and went in to say goodbye to Jonathan for the day, but he was asleep. She turned around after saying goodbye to Tim and walked down the stairs to go home. Nancy smiled at Susan as she still stood at the rail looking up at the beautiful, spacious cathedral ceilings. She was mentally imagining how she could BE the joy God asks us to be in life.

After standing at the railing for a little bit longer, Nancy walked back into Jonathan's room. He looked so peaceful sleeping. Tim got up from sitting by Jonathan's bedside and stretched his legs.

Nancy walked over to Tim and nuzzled up to him. She reached her arms around him. "You're such a good man."

"What…what did I do?"

"You said exactly what Jonathan needed to hear. When you were telling him the story about Never Quits… that was a good thing. You're my hero and you're Jonathan's hero."

"I'm just a man doing the best I can."

Tim and Nancy stood there immersed in gratitude for God. He had inspired them to know how to create a happy memory in that moment.

"Let's go home. I'm tired and it's dinnertime. Can we have some fish? For some reason I have a taste for halibut."

Nancy smiled and said, "Sure."

They let go of each other's embrace but not before Nancy gave Tim a quick peck on the cheek.

"You're beautiful…" said Tim looking lovingly into her eyes for an instant, "when you're about to cook me a delicious fish dinner."

"Oh! You…" said Nancy spanking him lightly on the arm.

They walked back into Jonathan's room to say goodbye to their grandson for the day. As they left the boy's room for the night, they didn't see that Jonathan was moving his hand toward his cheek. Something good was happening. Jonathan was getting better.

# Chapter Fourteen
## The Final Transition

The next week Susan came in to review Jonathan's current status. Tim and Nancy met the coma whisperer downstairs in the conference room again.

"I just wanted to review where I think we are with Jonathan. So far here's what he can do. He can cry, he can smile, he can understand some basic options, calm himself, breathe through the nose, open his eyes, close his eyes, and to some extent he can relax his muscles. I'm sure there's other things he can do, too, but these are the things that are obvious to me. Is there something else either of you want to add to this list?"

Nancy and Tim were silent for a moment, thinking.

"He can watch TV; he can look right at me sometimes and he can listen to a story being told him." said Tim.

"He responds well to cheek stroking. That really calms him down and helps him focus. If you ask him to smile as a way to tell us if he'd like something, he can do that."

"Of course! It's good that Jonathan's got such a great team of observers and caregivers. Here's what he can't do. Say letter "A". Do either of you want to add something to the list of what he can't do that he's been asked to do?"

"He can't do something for long periods of time. His stamina is still weak when it comes to relearning." said Tim.

"Right. These are things that are obvious to us. Because I want to work with what seems obviously easy for him to do, I'm going to ask him to use eye blinks to answer simple yes or no questions. The more we keep doing constructive things he CAN do, the more we improve the quality of his life. That is my goal." said Susan.

"When you say improve the quality of his life, do you think he'll ever completely recover?" asked Nancy.

"That's a great question. I can say that I feel very encouraged, but that's really a medical question. I can do nothing medical for him. I'm focused on supporting what the doctors can do for him. I can only focus on reducing stress and helping with improved communication. I think that he will continue to experience learning plateaus in what he can do. Like I said, because I can do nothing medical for him, I'd like to continue focusing on improving the quality of his life by doing what we've been doing. The doctors are the ones that know where the brain damage is. So, I encourage you to ask the doctors what they think he's capable of doing as far as completely recovering. What do you think about his stress reduction and communication efforts progress so far?"

"I think God is continuing to bless him with miracles daily. I feel hopeful he will recover completely." said Nancy.

"Me, too. Especially cheek stroking. It's amazing how that works so well." said Tim.

"I agree. I'm glad he found a way to communicate with us and calm himself using hypnotic suggestion."

There was a pregnant pause. Then Susan said, "How would you feel about praising God for healing Jonathan thus far?"

"It's a wonderful idea." said Tim.

Susan said, "Okay then, Tim. Would you like to offer a prayer of gratitude to God?"

Tim smiled and said, "I'd be honored to thank God."

The three of them bowed their heads and joined in praise for Jonathan's progress. After the prayer Susan said, "Well, let's see if Jonathan's up to receiving even more healing from God now."

With that, they went up to Jonathan's room. Susan wanted to see how open Jonathan might be to developing a talent for eye blinking as a simple conscious communication response.

Tim and Nancy stood by the right side of Jonathan's bed. Susan sat down on the right side of Jonathan's bed. He lay on his left side with his right side up. Susan leaned over his body up by his head speaking softly into Jonathan's right ear.

"Jonathan, hello this is your friend Susan. Jonathan, hello this is your friend Susan. Jonathan, hello this is your friend Susan." After a few seconds delay in Jonathan consciously responding with his eyes still closed, Susan moved her right hand to his right cheek and gently stroked it. She spoke softly into his ear saying the standard cheek stroking empowerment hypnotic suggestion. "Jonathan, every time your cheek is stroked instantly it's easy for you to think happy thoughts and to do what you'd like to do to feel powerful and happy."

After Susan spoke softly to him and stroked his cheek, Jonathan opened his eyes. Susan looked into Jonathan's eyes to get his attention.

"Jonathan, hello this is your friend Susan. Jonathan, hello this is your friend Susan. Jonathan, hello this is your friend Susan." Jonathan smiled looking right at her.

"Hello Jonathan, it's Susan. I'm here to teach you something new. If that's all right with you, give me one of your dazzling smiles."

Jonathan smiled one of his famous smiles. Susan smiled back at Jonathan.

"That's a very nice smile. What I'd like you to do today is to ask you to use your talent for eye blinking to answer simple "yes" and "no" questions. Do you like that idea? If you like that idea, show me a smile."

After a few seconds, Jonathan smiled again.

"Great! Here's what we'll do and the reason were doing it. I want to help you some more. We will ask you questions. We know you can open your eyes. Can you blink your eyes?"

Tim and Nancy stood by watching and listening as Susan continued to work with Jonathan. She opened and closed her eyes several times. "Jonathan, I just opened and closed my eyes several times. Jonathan, I just opened and closed my eyes several times. When you open and close your eyes several times people call that eye blinking. I opened and closed my eyes several times so you know what blinking looks like."

Jonathan seemed confused while he looked at Susan blinking her eyes.

"If you understand that opening and closing your eyes is called blinking, give me a smile."

Jonathan smiled after a short time.

"Is it easy for you to blink your eyes open and closed? If it is easy for you to blink your eyes, give me a smile."

Jonathan smiled though he looked like he was starting to feel tired.

"Would you blink your eyes open and closed for me one time?"

Jonathan opened and closed his eyes one time.

"That's great, Jonathan." said Susan. "What you just did by opening and closing your eyes is called eye blinking. If you understand that opening and closing your eyes is called eye blinking, blink your eyes one time."

Jonathan blinked his eyes one time.

"You've done a lot of hard work right now. If you would like to rest or even go to sleep right now, blink your eyes one time. When you blink your eyes one time you are telling me that you would like me to let you rest now."

Jonathan blinked his eyes one time.

"That's very good Jonathan. Thank you for talking with me and letting me know you need some rest now. Your grandma, grandpa and I are going to let you sleep now. We will be back later. If you understand blink your eyes one time."

Jonathan blinked his eyes once.

Nancy clasped her hands together in front of her chest excitedly. Tim stood on the left side of Nancy. He put his right arm around her beaming at Jonathan's progress.

"Snorrrrrrzzzzzz…" quietly came a sound from Jonathan.

"That was a lot of work for him to do." said Susan softly to Nancy and Tim. "He's obviously determined to get better. That's very good."

"Let's let him sleep now." said Nancy. Tim nodded his head. Susan got up and the three adults left Jonathan's room and walked out into the hall outside of Jonathan's hearing range.

"I'm going to create a healing visualization for him. I'll ask him to visualize rebuilding his body one section at a time. He's got a powerful mind and he's doing very nicely being able to consciously respond. Does he understand about using Popsicle sticks to build things?"

"He has built projects out of Popsicle sticks before." confirmed Nancy.

"I'm going to ask him to pretend his body is made of Popsicle sticks. In the visualization, I'll ask him to use his imagination and pretend that he's got a crew of helpers that can find the broken Popsicle sticks within him. Then, I'll ask him to imagine that this helping crew is assisting him in replacing all the broken Popsicle sticks within him so that he can get better. Then, I'll also ask him to pretend that the crew figured out how to connect a powerful magic battery to the Popsicle sticks. I'll ask him to pretend that the battery is giving power to all the replacement Popsicle sticks so that he can completely heal himself. Do you think he'll do that?"

"I think he'll do that if he wants to get better. I know he really likes to go fishing with me. So maybe you could ask him to pretend that when he gets all better, he gets to go on a fishing trip with me so that we can see if we can finally catch that old rascally Never Quits." said Tim.

"Great idea. It will give him something to look forward to." said Susan. "After I create this third hypnosis tape for him, you will have three customized recorded hypnosis programs you can play to help him continue to get better."

"Thank you so much for helping us get through to our grandson." said Nancy.

"He's got a way to go yet, but I feel encouraged. Hypnotic suggestion is an amazing tool he's open to using. Being a child and willingly using his vivid imagination really makes a huge difference for him. People who WANT to get better are the ones most likely to get better." said Susan.

"Thank goodness for that!" said Nancy.

"You said most likely?" wondered Tim.

"Yes, most likely. There are no guarantees of anything happening with hypnosis. As I've said all along, everything is up to Jonathan and God. So far, it looks as though Jonathan and God both want Jonathan to still be here for a while. I have no control over what God wants for Jonathan." said Susan. "Absolutely everything is up to God."

Nancy sighed a deep sigh. "I know what you just said is true."

"See you in a few days. I'll bring the healing visualization hypnosis program back with me and Jonathan can start listening to it. In the meantime, I encourage you and the staff to use what you've learned so far to communicate with Jonathan. Include using a smile and one eye blink to get confirmed conscious responses when communicating with him. Keep using the cheek stroking and the cheek stroking hypnotic suggestion to help him see how to empower himself and solve his challenges as they come up."

"All right, Susan. See you in a few days then." said Nancy.

Susan said goodbye to Nancy and Tim. Everything was moving in a positive direction for Jonathan. Things were getting better all the time.

After Susan created the third customized hypnosis program and recorded it for Jonathan, she gave the tape to Jonathan's grandparents. Nancy and Tim made sure their grandson listened to the healing visualization program on a regular basis. During Susan's next visit the following month the medical staff and Jonathan's family members felt amazed at the boy's progress.

During the next visit, Susan spoke once again to the boy. "Hi, Jonathan." said Susan. She sat next to Jonathan's bed visiting with him. It was her first visit with him after he had been listening to the healing visualization program for over a month.

Jonathan opened his eyes and looked right at Susan. He smiled broadly instantly recognizing her.

"He seems so much calmer, and happier." said Nancy. "Last week, Rose was here with him reading a story to him. I'm sure the hypnosis is making a big difference. She told us that he was moving his hand to his own cheek. He was having a bout of nausea and vomiting. After he moved his hand to his own cheek, I think that helped his nausea because he stopped vomiting."

Susan looked at Jonathan. "Did you do that? Did you make your nausea and vomiting go away by stroking your cheek? Wow! You are powerful!"

Jonathan smiled. He looked very pleased with himself. Though he still couldn't talk, he was using the power of his own mind to improve the quality of his life.

"Well, I'm glad I heard this news," said Susan. "It seems like Jonathan is really doing well. This makes it easier for me to share some news of my own."

"What's that?" asked Tim.

"My husband has gotten a job transfer. And we're going to be moving from Washington state to Virginia. It looks like the timing of this is perfect because Jonathan is doing so well."

"It doesn't sound like good news to me." started Tim. "How are we going to get along without you?"

"Well, Tim, I've really done about all I can to help Jonathan. You have three customized and recorded hypnosis scripts for our young hero here. As long as he continues to listen to those recordings, the rest is really up to God and Jonathan." said Susan. "I will give you my new address once I get it. Of course, we'll stay in touch."

"Of course, we're glad for you, Susan. But we're sad for us. Is this a promotion for your husband?" asked Nancy.

"He'll be working for a new company and yes, it is a promotion. Things will be good for you, too. If Jonathan needs a new hypnosis script, I can just mail it to you. And of course, you will continue to have the support of the HWH staff."

"Of course, it's going to be all right." agreed Nancy.

Tim somberly walked out of the room and down the stairs.

"There was no easy way for me to share that news with you." said Susan.

"Goodness, he has always been resistant to change. This has been quite an experience. I think he's just afraid of having to continue this without you." said Nancy.

"Well," said Susan, "if you need me, you'll be able to get a hold of me when I get my new address. I really mean that."

"I know. It will be fine. He just needs some time alone to deal with it in his own way. If he were younger, he would be climbing up to the top of the tree right now and communicating with God about it. It will be okay. He'll deal with it. When do you leave?"

"We've already sold our home to the new company. The movers come next week."

"Goodness. That was fast."

"Well, like I said," said Susan, "I knew there was no easy way to say this. We've been preparing and packing already for several days."

"We do wish you the best and are very grateful for all your help."

"I appreciate the opportunity I had to work with Jonathan and you and Tim. I've learned a lot about how to communicate with people in persistent vegetative state using hypnosis. Thanks for being open to letting me work with Jonathan."

"Again, thank you. You made a huge difference in our lives. Will you be back before you move?"

"I don't know. I'll play it by ear."

Nancy stood there looking at Susan not knowing what else to say.

"I'll see if I can find Tim on my way out. I'll figure out something to say to him."

Susan smiled. She waved goodbye to Nancy and walked out of Jonathan's room.

Susan headed downstairs to find Tim and to say a final goodbye. She found him standing and looking out a huge picture window that faced some majestic pine trees that were in the backyard of HWH.

"Tim," started Susan, "I'm sorry I dropped that news bomb on you so unexpectedly. I didn't really know how to say it any other way than the way I said it."

"What if Jonathan dies in the meantime? What if there could've been one more hypnosis script you could've written that could have extended his life even longer than it already did?"

"Hypnosis can't rewrite God's plan for anybody. God allowed us all to have this experience with Jonathan and hypnosis because that was part of God's plan for Jonathan and us. And anyway, I'm not the one that was writing hypnosis scripts. It was always God guiding me. So, God wrote the hypnosis scripts. I just wrote them down on paper. And as far as Jonathan dying, I have no control over that."

Tim shot a dark look at Susan. He didn't want to hear what she had just said.

Susan walked closer to Tim and said, "There's no telling when God is going to call us back home. Remember, Tim, what the pastor has always told us at church… we are spiritual beings having a human experience. Stop thinking like a human for a moment and consider the inevitable. Eventually, the human part of us will die. But the word 'die' has an unfair reputation. There is nothing scary about dying. Instead, it's a natural part of the human journey."

Tim refused to look at Susan. He just kept staring out the picture window looking at the pine trees. The wind was dancing in the treetops.

"Life with Jonathan has been a courageous journey for us all. I'm sure there's a part of you that knows the inevitable outcome is going to be physical body death. But look at how far you've come. When I first met you, you felt afraid Jonathan was going to die. As you changed your focus to what you could do to improve the quality of his life, you improved the quality of your life, too. You know you did!"

"If you're going to go, just go."

"Not until I'm finished. All of us have been on a journey together. This journey has been about never giving up. It's been about finding a way to respect ourselves as we have dealt with each of Jonathan's challenges. Even when we have thrown temper tantrums about feeling frustrated that we couldn't have our way FOR Jonathan, we have learned to accept the finite nature of human life."

Tim turned and finally looked toward Susan. He knew she had his best interests at heart.

"Part of this journey has been about accepting that some things just can't be fixed AND that the situation may be already as good as it gets. Together, we've experienced hills and valleys of what we all must weather during the finite life of a human. And anyway, we are all dying from the moment we are born. But the beauty of the experience is that when we are fully present in the now moment, we create happy memories. So, I encourage you in this now moment to keep creating a happy memory for Jonathan because right now he is very alive."

"I don't want you to go. There. Are you happy now?"

Susan chuckled. "There's a part of me that wants to stay, too. However, I don't think my husband would like that."

Tim sheepishly looked at Susan and said, "No, I don't suppose he would."

"You're going to be all right. You ARE going to get through this. I know things are challenging but the human experience is made up of challenges because I think that's what God wants for us. If everything was easy, what would be the purpose of experiencing life? That would be like being given a test and someone sneaking the answers to us. It would have very little value."

Tim reached his hand out to shake Susan's hand goodbye. "I shall surely miss you."

"And I will miss you." said Susan. "Listen, Tim, we ALL only have a limited amount of time to do meaningful things. You have a great influence over Jonathan… more than you know. Keep doing all the things that you're doing for him. Because you are reaching out and spending time with him you are creating the happiest possible memories for yourself, Nancy and him. And that's what makes life priceless."

"I guess I still feel guilty about being with Phil when the accident happened. If I could have, I would have stopped it from happening."

"Tim, I don't think God wanted you to stop this from happening. I think the accident was supposed to happen as a part of Jonathan's divine growth. Remember, Jonathan is a spiritual being having a human experience. As a part of that human experience, I think God arranges for us to be involved in situations that we would have never humanly agreed to sign on for. That's how we grow. This accident wasn't really about you. It was about Jonathan being able to grow."

"That's a hard concept to grasp." said Tim.

"You are a success, a winner, a priceless child of God. Just because you couldn't stop the accident from happening doesn't mean you have unsuccessfully met this challenge. I believe you are doing exactly what God wants you to do to help Jonathan grow spiritually. Being unable to change things in ONE situation because you thought it needed to be changed does NOT mean YOU are a total failure at life. It just means you were unable to have things the way YOU think they should be when God wants them to be another way for the involved person's highest Divine purpose."

"That sounds pretty deep."

"Go back upstairs, Tim. Nancy and Jonathan need you. Everything is gonna be okay. Just keep being there for them. When you are there for them, you're also there for you."

Tim looked intensely into Susan's eyes. "Is it all right if I hug you goodbye?"

Susan hesitated. She wasn't really a hugger, but she made an exception for Tim. The two friends respectfully embraced for a moment. They both knew Susan probably wouldn't be back. Then, without Tim looking at her, he let go and found his way back upstairs. Susan let herself out HWH's back door to go back home and continue packing.

Weeks morphed into months and months morphed into more than two years. Eventually, the brain damage could no longer sustain Jonathan's life. On March 25, 1993, Jonathan Wallace's life completed its cycle and he peacefully returned to his Heavenly home passing on in his sleep. Hypnosis had played an integral part in improving the quality of life of a young boy with loving grandparents.

# FINAL NOTES

Funerals Consumers Alliance (FCA) (www.funerals.org) is a non-profit organization that works to protect consumer's rights to choose meaningful, dignified and affordable funeral arrangements. This organization is like the Consumer Reports magazine for funeral purchases. Please visit their website for any details you might want to know about becoming a member.

The Fox family became lifetime members of this organization in 1988 before our son Jason died. FCA made it possible for us to afford Jason's burial. Joining the FCA is highly recommended should you want an affordable way for your end of earth life arrangements.

This organization made it possible for us to talk with Jason and write out on paper the way he wanted his end of earth life arrangements to go. That's one of the things they provide for you. They give you paperwork and you write out what you want done whether it be a funeral or a cremation. This greatly helps the survivors know what your end of earth life wishes are. The FCA negotiates special contracts with local funeral homes near you at reasonable prices.

When it was time for Jason's end of earth life arrangements, volunteers came and very respectfully took care of Jason's physical body. These people were very supportive and compassionate. I have nothing but good things to say about them. Everything was handled very professionally. I was so pleased with the way things were handled, that's why I am donating a portion of the proceeds of the sale of every copy of this book to them. – Susan Fox

Testimonials about Susan Fox's coaching

Susan Fox's *The Coma Whisperer* echoes the multitude of challenges caregivers face when supporting a loved one through a crisis. The case recounted in this book demonstrates the power of hypnosis, helping to improve the quality of life of a brain-injured youth and bring comfort, peace and hope to his caregivers. The author's personal experience as a caregiver, as well a hypnosis professional, combine to make a book that is both emotionally engaging and a valuable tool.

*Connie Hollett, Trained & Certified Consulting Hypnotist*
*Halifax, Nova Scotia, Canada*
++++++++++++

"The Coma Whisperer" by Susan Fox is a must read for anyone who needs comforting, acceptance and creative learning in their role as a caregiver. Sometimes, fate changes our lives in one dramatic moment and this story gives us many helpful ideas for how-to cope with situations that tax us and test our faith to the very core. Susan's story easily explains how each of us already possess the power of our mind through hypnosis and how natural it is; and at the same time reminding us that God has a divine plan for each of us that we may not comprehend. Hypnosis is a tool that allows us to expand our own personal growth when we are forced to face difficulties. I hope you enjoy "The Coma Talker" as much as I did. I plan on absorbing and practicing the lessons in my life right now!

Jane Ann Clemens, PMT, NCH, CHt Ben Lomond, CA
http://janeannmassagepro.blogspot.com/
++++++++++

A heartbreaking and heartwarming story of the power of love, the brain and God. Touching wisdom within inspires the reader. A must-read for anyone with a family member or friend with a long-term illness. Susan Fox has written an outstanding book that brings the hypnotism profession to a new level. At times, she teaches scientific concepts in an easy way for people to grasp. She uses storytelling to get her point across in an interesting way. Susan explains what hypnosis really is in an extraordinary way, perhaps the best I have ever heard. Finally, reading this book brings you more in touch with our spiritual purpose on this planet and I highly recommend it to everyone.

Beverly Keyes Taylor, CH
Homestead, Florida
www.easykeytolife.com
+++++++++++++++

The Coma Whisperer is skillfully written, moving and insightful. It had me choking back the tears as well as rejoicing for the future. Susan clearly demonstrates what an important and powerful tool hypnosis can be, as well as her unwavering trust in God.

Leslie Bonnick, Hypnotherapist, Axminster, UK
+++++++++++++++++

The hearing is the last to go. Coma victims can hear everything that is happening around them. Susan shows us the importance of staying strong and positive around unconscious patients. She connects us with the grandparents as they adjust to the tragic accident that caused their young grandson to slip into a coma. It was almost too much to bare after having buried their only son and daughter-in-law a few years back. We learn from their strength, positive attitude, and willingness to try an unconventional method to reach their grandson. Using Hypnosis Susan was able to give young Jonathan the gift of communicating with the hospital staff and his family. I highly recommend this book for anyone interested in knowing about alternative methods, finding inner strength during times of adversity, and the power of love and mindful living. This book is a must-read for hospital staff of coma patients and family members with loved ones in a coma.

Joyce Kostakis
+++++++++++++++

My name is Dorothy Morales. I'd like to tell you about a real event that happened in 2006. My friend's 42-year-old daughter, Sharon, became ill with colon cancer. During Sharon's illness, she eventually lapsed into a coma. Sharon used to call me Dottie.

Her body was at her mother's (June) house in Mansfield, Ohio. On the night before Sharon died, my friend, Sue Fox, called June. Sharon's spirit visited Sue who lived 45 minutes away in Fredericktown, Ohio. Sue said that Sharon was feeling nervous about crossing over. Sue works in palliative care and is used to spiritual visitations with people who are about to cross over.

Sue educated Sharon's spirit form about the crossing over experience. She explained to Sharon that when her spirit body completely comes out of her physical body, it would be painless. But Sharon felt anxious and worried about just letting go. So, Sue called June on the telephone.

Sue told June that Sharon's spirit was at Sue's house. Sue asked June how Sharon's physical body was behaving. June told Sue that Sharon's physical body, while still in the coma, was restless. So, Sue coached June on what to say to Sharon so Sharon could relax and let nature take its course. Sue asked June to hold on to one of Sharon's hands. June did that. Then, Sue started coaching June telling her the specific comforting words to say to Sharon's comatose body. Sue knows that the spirit hears everything, even during surgery when someone is in anesthesia.

After Sue coached June, and June said the words to Sharon, June said, "I just felt her body relax." And then Sue thought Sharon would finally cross over. So, Sue went to sleep. It was about 10pm or so after she hung up the phone with June.

But Sue says that Sharon came back. Her spirit visited Sue at about 1:30am the next morning. Sharon's spirit awakened Sue from a sound sleep.

Sue went into her living room so as not to wake her husband. When she was in the living room, she coached Sharon's spirit one more time about what would happen during the crossing over event. Sue had been emailing me and June because Sharon's spirit kept showing up at Sue's. She was talking with Sue about feeling different feelings during her illness.

Eventually, Sue says, that she saw Sharon's spirit cross over and disappear into nothingness. It was 1:50am on Sue's clock. After Sharon's spirit left, Sue went back to bed.

Sue called me the next morning about 10:30 am or so to see Sharon's status. I told Sue that Sharon had died at 1:50am.

As Sue was sharing this spiritual experience about Sharon with me, Sue said, "Oh Sharon is here talking to me right now. She says, 'Tell Dottie not to cancel her trip to Colorado.' I felt amazed to hear Sue say this because SHARON DID NOT KNOW I was taking this trip!!!! I did not tell Sharon directly that I was going. Because of what Sue said, that was how I knew Sue was really talking with Sharon's spirit.

It was also interesting to hear this message because in fact, I was feeling guilty going away and not being at Sharon's Memorial service, as we all knew Sharon was dying. But Sharon told me to go ahead and go to Colorado as I had planned!!! I know Sue Fox really talked with Sharon.

Dorothy Morales  R.N.
Mansfield, Ohio
++++++++++++

I received a phone call that Tina, a mutual friend of mine and Susan's, was in the hospital. I went to the hospital. The medical professionals told me she was unconscious. Since Tina couldn't talk, I sat and waited and prayed over her for 17 days for her return to consciousness.

After praying about 2 weeks, I called Susan and told her that Tina was in a coma. Susan came to the hospital. Together we put our hands on Tina and did Jin Shin Jyutsu as Susan instructed me to do.

Then, I did the Jin Shin Jyutsu flows Susan showed me one more time by myself the next day, March 30, 2009. The next day, Tina came out of the coma.

I believe that prayer and the Jin Shin Jyutsu caused Tina's miraculous return.

Sue Ellyn Wiggand
Centerburg, Ohio
+++++++++++

## A Night's Message in the Life of Susan Fox

I met Susan Fox, a remarkable intelligent woman, at an evening talk she presented at the National Guild of Hypnotists (NGH) conference in Marlborough, MA. in 2006. Susan made a strong impression on me with the detailed demonstrations she used to display the uniqueness and power of the four very individual points of view of the four human brain quadrants, and how, as a Hypnotist, we could engage and get results most effectively with each brain quadrant viewpoint.

At the end of the conference, I looked forward to seeing Susan at the next NGH Conference. But the four thinking styles of the brain continued to intrigue me, so after the conference I took a course which Susan offered in BrainView Training. Through the BrainView Training course I got to know Susan a little better, and realized that beyond her experience with brain function research, Susan was also well trained in the subtle energy rebalancing work of Jin Shin Jyutsu, and Susan was gifted in her natural talent of psychic connection with those who had passed.

The following year after Susan and I had struck up a friendship, we arranged to share accommodation with friends at the 2007 NGH Conference. The conference proceeded as usual. Then, the evening prior to Susan's presentation on Saturday morning, only the two of us were in our hotel room. And, something unexpected happened. After preparing to turn in for the evening, Susan had gone to bed. I finished the paperwork I'd been doing, and as I got ready to get into my bed I remember taking a moment to notice the moonlight shining in through the hotel room window was lovely, and felt peaceful after a busy day.

I was about to turn off the lamp near my bed on the nightstand, when I realized that Susan seemed to be talking in her sleep. The words Susan was speaking seemed more than mumbled words, and I thought for a moment that she may have been speaking to me. Susan slowly sat upright, and put her legs over the edge of the bed as she continued speaking quietly. I couldn't hear clearly what she was saying, so I began to focus on actively listening to the words spoken. I sat forward to make eye contact, but Susan didn't seem aware of me at all. In fact, as I looked more closely at her, it seemed that Susan was in an altered state. It crossed my mind that perhaps Susan was a sleep-walker, and I looked for signs to see if that might be true.

Susan's body appeared to be 'in neutral' and that while it was Susan was speaking, it seemed to me that Susan acted unaware of speaking or taking any action. She did not show any sign of consciousness, yet the oddest part to me was what Susan seemed to be saying. The words were spoken by Susan, but also seemed to be from another person or persons unseen. The words were not random, but rather a disjointed conversation with people invisible to me.

I realized at this point that Susan was saying clearly she wanted to leave. To leave now. There was a delay then the reply came that she was not to go. Susan insisted that it was too much, that she had done all she could do on her own. The reply came again that it was not time, and she (Susan) had more to do. More silence. And that she could do it. I think she asked for help, but there was no clear reply.

Words which floated out into the room were without any seeming emotional intensity. As I realized the meaning of the words, I felt uncomfortable, like a trespasser in witnessing such a personal exchange as what was unfolding before me.

It seemed that more time passed than the words I can remember hearing might have actually taken to speak. But the feeling in the room was *altered* – and even after the words stopped the altered feeling continued. Susan also continued to seem to be unaware of her surroundings in the hotel room.

After a few minutes of silence when I asked Susan if she was all right, she seemed to come back fully into the focus of the room we were in. She said yes she was all right. Susan seemed to wonder how she had gotten to be on the edge of the bed, and she asked if she had been speaking out loud. When I said she had seemed to be having a conversation with others I could not see, she explained it had already been a challenging year, and told me a few personal details which helped to make sense of what I had heard.

We talked for a while of how people receive information from their spirit, guardian angels, or wise mind. When we had talked for a time, and the space around us seemed normal and peaceful again, we both went to our respective beds, and the night passed without further incident.

Janice Smylie, Ph.D.
++++++++++++++

## Susan Knew My Mom Had Crossed Over Before I Told Her

I met Susan Fox at an event in 2008 that another friend was hosting in the fall after my mother's death. Susan was the guest speaker on Ho'Oponopono. Ho'ponopono is a Hawaiian prayer technique used by thousands of people to bring peace and healing to them. I had never heard of Ho'Oponopono and was curious to know more. Little did I know that decision would change my life forever. My mom had died of breast cancer the year before and as I watched her health deteriorate, I wanted to know if there was another way to heal the body without using traditional Western medicine. Following my mom's death, I felt a strong need to embark on a new spiritual journey that could answer these questions and many more.

I was a "newbie" on my spiritual journey when I met Susan and still wasn't sure what I believed at that point in time. I had been raised by Christian parents and grandparents that had passed on strong Christian beliefs to me; and I was unwilling to ignore those beliefs. I had considered trying to connect with my mom in spirit world prior to meeting Susan, but I was still too scared and not certain that it was all real.

Following Susan's presentation, I approached her to ask a question. She answered my question and then asked me a few questions. Then she unexpectedly said to me, "Your mom is here in this room right now and she is standing next to you with her arm around your shoulders." I was in complete shock because I never told her my mom was dead.

I didn't know what to say. Susan asked me if I wanted to know what my mom wanted to say to me. I remember thinking "Is this real?" I slowly said, "Yes..." (with much hesitation).

I don't recall exactly what Susan said next, but it was something like, "Your mom says she loves you very much and wants you to let go of the pain of her death and move on with your life." I was in complete shock because this is something I would "expect" my mom to say.

Then Susan had to leave the room to go outside and get something from her car. I was still trying to decide if what Susan had said to me was real or not, when Susan returned to the room and said to me, "Your mother has more to say, do you want to hear it?" I spent the next 15 minutes listening to things my mom wanted me to know.... all through Susan.

When Susan was finished I was in such "complete peace" and overcome with joy because I knew I had let go of my pain about mom dying and moved on. I had never experienced anything like that before and it had happened so spontaneously that I did not have much time to comprehend what was happening until it was over.

Susan taught me a simple technique for talking with my mom. It requires you to center your mind and heart into a peaceful, loving memory first. Then, you place your hands palm up in your lap. Susan talks with the deceased loved one and sets up a simple way of communicating between the living person and the deceased loved one.

Susan asked my mom to answer simple yes or no questions by waving her spirit hands over my physical hands. I would ask a question following Susan's system then mom would answer 'yes' or 'no' according to Susan's simple technique. I quickly could feel the energy changes over my hands as mom answered. And, I knew without a doubt that it was mom doing it. Susan also set up a symbol between me and my mom. When I see that symbol, I know it is Mom talking to me.

Somehow Susan can hear and see them. I don't know how she does it but beyond any doubt, I know she can do it.

There was no doubt in my mind following that day that I could indeed talk to my mom... and it would be real. Since that day, I have talked to my mom in spirit world countless times. She sometimes comes to me in my dreams or sometimes through a bird or small animal that I see in my yard. I will say to the animal, "Hi mom, I see you!" to let her know that I acknowledge she is around me.

I never talk to the rest of my family about these things because they would probably have me locked up! I still miss my mom every day, but it does bring me much comfort to know she is so close and I can talk to her whenever I want.

This is a gift that Susan introduced me to and something that helped me get past my fear of "communicating with dead people!" I will forever be grateful to Susan for her amazing abilities.

Denise Musser
++++++++++++

## Natural Calming During A Nasty Divorce

"After being an energy field student of Susan Fox's, I am more aware of my energetic life. I've learned how to use the things I've learned from her classes and private consultations to tap into my natural ability to heal, genuinely love and improve the quality of my relationships.

Recently one of my children went through a nasty divorce. He became a single dad for 4 children. I stepped in and helped them through this devastating experience. I realized I was using energy field training with my grandchildren to calm them during this very stressful time.

The things I've learned from Susan are not a mindset thing. They are real! Everything really does boil down to knowing how to tap into the energy fields all around us. I highly encourage anyone wanting to learn how to be happy using knowledge of their human energy field to attend any of Susan's trainings or privately consult with her. It will be one of the best things you've ever done in your life!"

Sandy T.
++++++++

## Expert Intuitive

"In my personal and professional experience in working with Sue Fox, I have found it to be a very enlightening and enjoyable experience. Her knowledge and expertise in a vast number of areas enhance her teaching skills and ability to project her teachings to her students.

I have attended a number of her classes and instructional technique modes and used them often in real life situations. When I first met her I had no idea where she came from. When the students are ready the teacher appears. She certainly brought information applicable and pertinent for my daily life experience and I continue to use it this day.

Her integrity and professional approach are excellent. She uses her intuitive nature and skills to resolve issues more quickly than any other practitioner I know."

Linda C.
+++++++++

## Before I Asked, She Knew What I Needed

"This morning I was thinking that I needed some money to do laundry in the college dorm laundry machines. That was about 11 o'clock. At about 1'oclock Mom called me (Susan) to say she had just put some money in my bank account. She told me that a little earlier around 11 o'clock or so she felt like I had asked her to put some money in the bank for me. I didn't even use the telephone but she got the message anyway. Thanks, Mom."

Keenan Fox
+++++++++

I am a member of a natural health and wellness chat room on Skype. Many people share their talents in this chat room. Susan is one of those people.

One morning, I texted the room that my sister had just died. Susan answered my text explaining that she was an alternative health stress management specialist. With patience and calm,

Susan shared simple, non-medical ideas about how I could reduce my stress during this very stressful time for me.

During this difficult time it was hard to think clearly due to my emotional state from the death of my sister. Susan was there for me. She kept texting and even talked with me on the phone and on Skype. She has continued to follow up weeks after she initially answered my text.

Susan is the kind of person who will be there for you. She's a good listener and very non-judgmental. What a great friend I have made in her.

If anyone is open to complimentary medicine approaches for natural stress relief, you can be sure that Susan Fox would be a great coach for you.

Shae
(Tennessee)
+++++++++

I was absolutely stunned when Wayne's doctor alluded to me that there was little to no hope of recovery - the nature of the stroke had precluded use of the clot busting drug, and - news to me the day of his stroke - Wayne's left carotid artery was 100% blocked, and the clot ran the length of his neck; eliminating surgery as an option. The only hope was drug therapy, which they hoped would limit the damage; the specialist our family doctor had consulted with wasn't sure the drugs would have any effect, and my impression of what I was told was that this stroke was a one way street. All downhill.

At the end of that first long day, I quietly let a few friends know via private message and email about the stroke (our son had been on the phone most of the day notifying family) that ended with a simple request - "Ask for a miracle."

One of my good friends asked if she could post in a couple of groups, on my behalf, for healing to be sent our way and I agreed. Susan Fox, a complementary medicine stress management specialist in Ohio, contacted me a few days after the stroke, asking if I would be open to an alternative health method that naturally reduces stress for people in stroke. Susan contacting me was one of those miracles.

I had never posted anything on Facebook about Wayne having the stroke, and she is not a member of either of the groups my friend did post in - so how did she learn that we needed her help? I instantly said yes - I have a background in energy healing myself and know the power that our bodies have to heal, given the right tools.

Susan coached me on what to do to start healing and reopening the energy pathways in Wayne's body. It was wonderful to see him respond with improved movement and speech, many times within just a couple of hours of having worked with him following Susan's coaching. Wayne never completely lost his cognitive ability but his speech was basically reduced to 'yes' and 'no' for several days. His ability to communicate improved virtually every day even through the brain damage also caused aphasia.

The methods Susan uses are non-invasive, simple to carry out, and amazingly effective. The results are impressive. If you need help with pain or stress and tension relief please do your body good and contact her. You can read her blog and other testimonials at www.brainviewtraininginstitute.com. She's done some incredible work.

Janice McClelland
Caregiver (and Wife) for Wayne McClelland after his stroke
Manitoba, Canada
++++++++++++++

I had a stroke. Things went from bad to worse; the doctors didn't sound encouraging. I was dying and even if the doctors could prevent that, their 'best case' scenario wasn't much to look forward to. Somehow through Facebook this lady in the US learned of the stroke, contacted Jan and started instructing her on how to help me. I couldn't believe that I felt different - in a good way! - after Jan had done nothing more than touch different parts of my body. She says only a short time passed, sometimes only hours before there would be noticeable improvements, sometimes in movement, sometimes in my speech.

I didn't really understand what she was doing, or what 'it' was doing for me but on some level I knew it was important and would even remind Jan to do the energy work if it looked like she was going to leave for the day and we hadn't done it. I am grateful Susan helped me and is still helping me. I recommend Susan to anyone who needs help using alternative health methods for stroke recovery.

Wayne (Kenneth) McClelland
Stroke victim and recovering stroke miracle
Manitoba, Canada
+++++++++


## In Closing

Possibly the greatest gift we have been given is Eternal Life through the infinite Love of Our Creator. Every thought we think affects each of us. That is why thinking Loving thoughts can greatly improve the quality of every person's life everywhere.

So much about the brain is still unknown. However, we are learning more and more about ourselves. If we will think about the possibilities of Love, we will keep creating Loving solutions to life.

As I have experienced with the thousands of clients with whom I've worked since 1988, I believe each thought we think is a unique frequency. When we consciously tune into the frequency of Love and work from that viewpoint, we lovingly affect each other.

With this idea in mind, it is my belief that if you begin reading this book each time by first intentionally feeling the feeling of Love, you will attract that frequency more strongly into your experience with this book. Into your individual life situations, you will generate Loving solutions to you to create peace of mind.

Ground yourself into this feeling with every breath you breathe, with every thought you think. By doing this you BECOME Love.

I encourage you to embrace Love in all you do. Think LOVE at every waking moment. By thinking through the mindset, eyes and feelings of LOVE you will attract more and more of it TO you. THAT is how you BECOME Love into your human experiences.

Anything unlike Love runs away. You can repel violence, hatred and all things unlike Love simply by consciously CHOOSING to think of loving outcomes FIRST before anything else.

I ask you to use your brain's right hemisphere by imagining the possibilities of Love in all that you do. You do this simply by accepting ONLY Love images into your Life. The key to attracting Authentic, Genuine, Eternal Love is simply to Love.

Love is attracted to its own frequency. The more you Love, the more Love is attracted to you.

So, you might ask what that really means. That means when you think in critical, judgmental ways, you are attracting lack into your life. You are creating a reality of lack and poverty into your life. So, when you see something and notice that which you do not like, you are vibrating thoughts from your brain's left hemisphere which is where the Human version of You, the Eternal Spiritual Being, judge and criticize. Be mindful of the times you use your abilities to judge and criticize for they can be your undoing.

You are a powerful Spiritual ENERGY Being simultaneously experiencing a Human Experience on earth. Quantum theorists have done much research on this phenomenon.

You use your Spirit, the Eternal Version of YOU to ANIMATE the Human Being version of you on earth. You are only a Human on earth. Once you complete your earth experience, YOU, the REAL you, the Spiritual, Eternal YOU returns to your Etheric home free of the very dense Human version, You that has an individual name easily identifiable by other humans while on the earth. Once the Real You is done vibrating and animating its human energy body while confined by earth energy laws and experiencing life as a human, the Real You is released from its human costume and returns home.

We are all connected by energy. With your thoughts you create your realities and your relationships. I encourage you to lead and live your life using your right brain. Do this and you attract to you genuinely Loving relationships. And life is all about the relationships we create. That is why the brain has four quadrants and creates relationships within itself.

Your brain is like a radio station broadcasting messages 24/7. Within your brain you actually have four unique ways of knowing, observing and identifying your life situations. It is by thinking your thoughts that you create and attract to you that which you think. Understanding this, I encourage you to 'see' life from constructive viewpoints, thinking about how you can improve the quality of life for those around you as well as yourself. Doing this is how you reach out and give, the same way Our Creator Eternally Gives us Life.

YOU, the Real You, the Spirit You thinks Love thoughts from your brain's right hemisphere. When the Human Version of you mimics the Real version of You, your Human life situations are wonderful.

With the spatial qualities found in your right brain you can attract to you all forms of Love. When you THINK anything wonderful is possible, the Universe arranges for wonderful possibilities to be your destiny. And, by using your brain's left abilities to constructively develop and contribute to life, you enrich your life instead of deny yourself rich life scenarios.

So, when you begin to notice yourself thinking and then saying critical and judgmental thoughts that detract from contributing to a wonderful life, you are 'tuning in' and attracting to you a world of mental poverty.

Think in constructive, contributory ways that include and encourage others to enjoy life. Doing so you can invent and give to life instead of detract from it. I encourage you to think in ways that give instead of take away as you read the following story based on actual events. Especially if you are a caregiver, think about how to improve life and that is what you create in your reality.

## Susan's Work Continues

Since working with Jonathan, I've been privileged to work with thousands of women experiencing some type of stress. I first started my hypnosis career working with students wanting to overcome their public speaking fears and the effects of test-taking freeze-ups. However, I've added several other ways to help clients get natural stress relief. These main techniques I use are Jin Shin Jyutsu (www.jsjinc.net), hypnosis, Reiki and chakra clearing. All these natural ways of reducing stress can help you improve your qualify of life, too.

I've worked with people in coma, stroke recovery, PTSD, fears, phobias, panic attacks and various tension stories. Often, we overlook the cumulative effects of tension. I encourage you to think about your own life and consider researching complementary health methods.

Another true-life story found on my website's marketplace is the The Personal Transformation Story of Wayne McClelland's Stroke Recovery. Briefly, Wayne's left carotid artery became 100% blocked. This blockage eliminated him from being eligible for the clot busting drug. Wayne's wife Jan looked to connect with anyone who might help with her husband's stroke. Essentially, doctors told Jan to take him home and prepare for the worst. Somehow, I learned about the situation although to this day Jan swears she never posted a message about Wayne's stroke. That's just one of the many miracles to this story.

Anyway, once Jan and I connected, I immediately started suggesting some things to her using something called Jin Shin Jyutsu. Within hours of using this universal art of relieving tension, Wayne started to recover from his stroke. Please stroll over to www.brainviewtraininginstitute.com and look at the marketplace. This book is available by instant download.

I've worked with many other people. If you are open-minded and searching for a stress relief coach, please email me at brainviewtraininginstitute@gmail.com.

Love,
Susan

www.ingramcontent.com/pod-product-compliance
Lightning Source LLC
Chambersburg PA
CBHW072003040426
42447CB00009B/1459